S0-BSD-253

CHRISTIAN
KNOWLEDGE
of GOD

James Harry Cotton

NEW YORK
The Macmillan Company
1951

211
C82C

First Printing

28426
Feb '53

ACKNOWLEDGMENTS

Acknowledgment is made to the following for permission to reprint from their
publications:

Adam and Charles Black, Ltd., for *Early Greek Philosophy* by John Burnet,
copyright 1930.

George Allen & Unwin, Ltd., for *The Christian Understanding of Man* by T. E.
Jessop, copyright 1938.

Burns Oates & Washbourne, Ltd., for *Summa Theologica,* copyright 1911. For
American rights: Reprinted from the *Summa Theologica of St. Thomas Aquinas,*
Vol. I, with the permission of Benziger Brothers, Inc., publishers and copyright
owners.

Burns Oates & Washbourne, Ltd., for *Modern Thomistic Philosophy* by R. P.
Phillips, copyright 1935; for American rights, The Newman Press, Westminster,
Maryland, copyright 1946.

The University Press, Cambridge, England, for *Philosophical Theology* by F. R.
Tennant, copyright 1937. The University of Chicago Press, for *The Source of
Human Good* by H. N. Wieman, copyright 1946, and *The Journal of Religion.*

E. P. Dutton & Co., Inc., for *A Treatise of Human Nature* by David Hume,
Everyman's Library, copyright 1920.

Harcourt Brace and Company, Inc., for *Modern Man in Search of a Soul* by C. G.
Jung, copyright 1933.

Harper & Brothers for *Antic Hay* by Aldous Huxley, copyright 1923; for *Religious
Perplexities* by L. P. Jacks, copyright 1923; for *The Nature of Religious Experience* by J. S. Bixler *et al.,* copyright 1937; for *Ends and Means* by Aldous
Huxley, copyright 1937; for *The Problem of Religious Knowledge* by D. C. Macintosh, copyright 1940; for *Is There a God?* by D. C. Macintosh, copyright
1932; for *American Philosophies of Religion* by H. N. Wieman and B. E.
Meland, copyright 1936; and for *The Bible: A New Translation* by James Moffatt, copyrighted by Harper & Brothers 1922–1935 and copyrighted 1950 by James
Moffatt, used by permission.

Harvard University Press for *Fugitive Essays* by Josiah Royce, copyright 1925, and
for *Attic Vase-Painting* by Charles T. Seltman, copyright 1933.

Hodder & Stoughton, Ltd., for *The Knowledge of God* by Karl Barth, copyright
1939.

*To my father and mother
who first led me to a
knowledge of God*

THE JAMES SPRUNT LECTURES

Mr. James Sprunt, of Wilmington, North Carolina, in 1911 established a perpetual lectureship at Union Theological Seminary in Virginia, which would enable this institution to secure from time to time the services of distinguished ministers and authoritative scholars as special lecturers on subjects connected with various departments of Christian thought and Christian work. The lecturers are chosen by the Faculty of the Seminary and a Committee of the Board of Trustees, and the lectures are published after their delivery in accordance with a contract between the lecturer and these representatives of the institution.

The series of lectures on this foundation for the year 1947 is presented in this volume.

B. R. Lacy, Jr.

PRESIDENT

*Union Theological Seminary
in Virginia*

Introduction

This book has grown out of a two-fold concern. The first is with our civilization, which is afflicted with a critical sickness. Wistfully, yet without much confidence, men are turning to the Christian faith, hoping that it may illumine the meaning of the crisis of our time and that it may provide some resources for meeting it. Yet men are not at all clear as to what they expect from Christian faith. Some hope to find moral vision and energy. Others frankly expect a religious revival to rescue various human institutions in which they have a personal interest. Others want comfort and encouragement in a world that has denied their best hopes. Some seek an authority that will provide a sure answer for their bewildering questions. They have been wearied by their lonely wrestle with the mysteries. Many have a pretentious confidence in the power of human reason, which is often a disguised confidence in themselves. The question which ought to trouble the minds of men is not how we can marshal the resources of religion to preserve our human institutions, but the far more momentous question of how we can come to a knowledge of God.

The second concern is with the Church. Both among the clergy and the laity there is widespread confusion about what faith really means. The pulpit is laboring hard, entreating, scolding, offering utopian hopes, prophesying in a confusing variety of tongues. One misses the great simplicities of the Christian faith and senses a loss of conviction that its basic insights are profoundly, grandly true. Many ministers are half apologetic of the Gospel which purports to be God's answer to human need. The laity are uncomfortable because they cannot speak with any confidence about their faith. To be quite honest, the Church ought to be deeply embarrassed by the inquiries of the modern mind. It ought to say, "We are sorry, gentlemen, but we are not at all clear ourselves about where we are going. We shall have to withhold our answer for a time until we can discover our own meaning." Among those who do have a clear knowledge of biblical religion, many are inarticulate because contemporary thought is quite foreign to them. They do not understand their contemporaries, nor can they make themselves understood. Long ago they surrendered large areas of thought and experience to the secular mind. Now they can only watch the growth of that mentality in sullen and helpless despair.

One of the central difficulties between faith and thought arises from defects in our theories of knowledge. Two general theories have been disputing the field between them. According to the one, knowledge is directed to concepts, or Plato's universals, and logic is the supreme test. According to the other, all knowledge is intensely practical, answers to biological and social interests, and the test is to be found in pragmatic working. Each party has argued with cogency and plausibility. It is possible that both are right, at least in what they affirm. We shall proceed in that direction.

We shall see that we can account for our knowledge of persons only by the union between what Josiah Royce called the external meaning and the internal meaning of ideas. The treatment of internal meaning is confessedly preliminary, with many of its implications yet to be developed. But much can now be claimed. For example, in our knowledge of others, it becomes clear that faith, which is the highest expression of internal meaning, and reason, which is the fulfillment of external meaning, are not alternate ways of knowing, but inseparable parts of one living whole. Here it is also evident that moral conditions are essential to knowledge. This opens a fresh approach to the knowledge of God, to the central place of revelation and the intensely personal nature of this highest knowledge. There can be no direct knowledge of God apart from that personal trust which is "pure in heart," that commits *all* our human concerns to the keeping of God. It follows that the skeptic can no longer regard this revelation and this trust as intellectual evasions.

This book aspires to stand in the Christian tradition. For this I offer no apology. It seems quite futile to take one's stand in the midst of some philosophical desert, where nothing is taken for granted, and to see how far one can travel from nowhere. For that matter, I have never read a book in philosophy in which no assumptions were made at the beginning. But one must also accept the obligation to state his case as rationally as possible, relating his claims to contemporary and competing interpretations. One can never be sure that he is fair to rival views, and I apologize for any failure at this point.

The argument falls at times into difficult places, although I have tried to write in non-technical language and without presupposing much detailed knowledge of philosophy or theology on the part of the reader. But such a study does demand both philosophical and theological interest, for the greatest concerns of human life are here involved. None but the valiant, who are made so by a persistent hunger for God and by the overpowering crisis of our time, can render service in the field of Christian thought.

I have also tried to make the treatment fairly complete for the general reader. The text has been almost entirely rewritten since the lectures were delivered. Chapters 2, 3 and 5 were not given at Richmond.

I cannot begin to acknowledge my debts incurred in writing this book. My heartiest thanks are given to President Lacy and the faculty of Union Theological Seminary in Richmond, Virginia, both for the invitation to give the James Sprunt lectures and for their complete hospitality during the week of the lectures; to several friends who have read the manuscript and made helpful criticisms; especially to Dr. William H. Hudnut of Rochester, New York, who has taken special care to be a faithful critic; to Dr. Harold B. Walker of Evanston, Illinois; to my former colleague, Professor R. Frederick West at Wabash College; to my present colleague, Professor Hans Frei; and to my wife who has read both the manuscript and the proofs and has helped greatly with many suggestions on style and content. *J. Harry Cotton*

Contents

CHAPTER I

The Dilemma of Faith

Christian faith is in a vexatious dilemma. What it has to say is momentous, yet it does not know how to speak. The language which it must use is shaped and adapted to the affairs of this world. Yet faith has something to say that seems strangely out of place in the world. The God whom faith declares surpasses not only our language but our forms of thought as well. A language adequate to faith's purpose would not make sense to the human mind. Our understanding is adapted to making tools, to building houses, to solving mathematical problems, and to probing the secrets of nature. God cannot be reduced to these terms. Yet faith must speak, even though incapable of speech. Faith is certain that, apart from God, human affairs are moving to swift destruction. It claims supreme wisdom; yet it cannot make its own case plausible.

This embarrassment is not new. The writers of the Bible labored under the same burden. They strained at the limits of human thought and language. God was beyond the power even of their imagination. They heard His question, "Where wast thou when I laid the foundations of the earth? Declare, if thou hast understanding." [1] They heard the prophet speaking on behalf of God, "To whom then will ye liken me, that I should be equal to him?" [2] They cried out with Paul, "O the depth of the riches and wisdom and knowledge of God! How unsearchable are his judgments and how inscrutable his ways!" [3] The long succession of the mystics, one after the other, have given up trying to describe what they have seen. You cannot apply to God any human predicate, however lofty, without falsifying what you say.

On the other hand, faith cannot keep silent without betraying itself. Any living faith, Christian or otherwise, becomes articulate. The devotee of a faith does not need to be argued into telling it. But to explain means to tell others what faith means. They have a right to ask searching questions: How do you know all this? Who is this God? What have I to do with Him? How may I find Him? You say He has spoken. Where and when? What are His unmistakable accents? When Moses was charged by God with the task of leading Israel out of Egypt, he anticipated such questions from his own people and from the Egyptians. "And they shall say to me, What is his name?" [4] "They will not believe me, nor hearken unto my voice; for they will say, Jehovah hath not appeared unto thee." [5] And the Pharaoh would say, "Who is Jehovah, that I should hearken unto his voice to let Israel go?" [6] When the evangelist goes to other lands, confronts people of other faiths, he must be even more articulate. Here he must attempt an answer to other questions: How and why does your gospel negate or fulfill that which we already believe? On what ground do you seek to win us from our ancestral gods and their ancient customs?

Throughout the world secular unbelief is challenging the very right of Christian faith to exist. This is no mere philosophic doubt, the issue of which might be settled by urbane argument. It is a positive and pervasive force, this organization of life apart from God. It is taken for granted by much modern literature, drama, even by the fine arts. It is implicit in man's daily struggle for existence. In political and economic encounters, the assumptions on which men habitually act do not take God into account. When a man enters the world of human affairs, he finds his fellows reckoning on power, political influence, wealth, human ingenuity, group loyalties, the half-gods of nation, race, and class. But God seems an impertinence. When the specific issue is raised men deny the fact of God; they do not see the need of anything resembling Christian salvation; and they insist that the Christian interpretation of man, of history, and of human destiny, is not relevant to contemporary life.

Or worse still, the fact of God is not explicitly denied. But belief in Him becomes a matter of individual taste, of private opinion. Religion is a symbolism, a kind of interior decoration. If a man finds any comfort in it, that is his own affair. No one disputes his right to this comfort any more than he is disposed to argue with a bride and groom over their taste in furniture. Let them beware only of trying to impose their taste on their neighbors! But this relegation of God to the position of a private symbol, the suspicion that faith does not point to outward fact, is the one thing which Christian faith cannot endure. The large company of modern thinkers who have argued, in one form or another, that faith is merely a subjective feeling, or a private option, these the Christian faith has rightly taken to be guilty of a deadly kind of flippancy. But faith cannot be flippant. It will not consent to trifling with the most serious concerns of the human soul.

The Christian Church cannot long be indifferent to this skepticism. It cannot pretend that it does not exist, or that it belongs to a small group of esoteric and generally harmless college professors. The doubt of God is in the very air that we breathe. It invades even the sanctuary. Quietly the "acids of modernity" have eaten conviction out of the Church. Without conviction, her life becomes formal, polite, and scarcely creates a ripple of disturbance in the affairs of the world.

Now when Christian faith tries to awaken conviction, it must appeal to reason. It means something. It intends an objective content about which something can be said. It enters the world of fact with the supreme Fact. But the world of fact is reason's domain. To relate one fact to another, and more especially to relate one meaning to another, is the work of reason. In explaining itself, in talking at all, faith relates its message to what is already known, or it talks nonsense. Let the record of man's reasoned attempts to find God be ever so unimpressive; let the meaning of

God be so majestic as to shatter the very forms of human thinking; let reason be conceived as perverted by sin, so that man is
incapable of understanding God without the special grace of
illumination; let man himself be conceived as irrational, reason
debased to the mean instrument of his passions; nevertheless, if
faith is to talk with serious intent, it seeks to convey meaning, to
make itself understood. Let religion despair of using reasoned
argument; let it appeal to conscience or stir the feelings; let it
resort to parable, to myth, to art, to music, to symbol; nevertheless,
faith seeks to say something. Faith points, even when it cannot
define. Faith despises vagueness, insists that its Object is definite
and actual. But in intending a definite content, in pointing to an
actual Being, faith makes its own appeal to meaning, that is, to
reason.

This dilemma is at the heart of Christian knowledge. We try
to escape it at our peril. If, on the one hand, we forget the im-
possibility of our task, we end by reducing God to human proportions, making Him too plausible to be believed. On the other
hand, if we give up the attempt to be rational, we end by shouting
our beliefs, or by repeating them—hoping to dull all opposition
by wearing it out; or professing to despise reason, we continue to
use it, and to use it badly. It is safe to say that no significant advance
toward the knowledge of God will be made except by men who
are content to find their very destiny in this dilemma.

Let us be clear that the dilemma is in no way artificial, that,
as Berkeley put it, we are not first raising a dust and then complaining that we cannot see. Faith has good grounds for its distrust of reason and cannot live within the limits that reason sets.
We shall first examine these grounds. Then we shall hear reason's
reply to faith and its exposure of faith's pretense that it can ever
live without reason. This treatment will serve at once to sharpen
the dilemma of faith and to clarify the issues that confront us.
First, then, let us hear the case of faith against reason.

1. The record of natural theology is not conclusive. Uncounted volumes have been written, seeking to prove the existence of God, or to establish the credibility of certain doctrines of the Christian faith. In most of these books it is clear that the interest of the writers, expressed in their own faith, sprang from sources other than the reasons they now offer. They are trying to bring men to believe in God by a road other than that they themselves have traveled. Some of this work has lasting importance and much of it has been of use to faith. But the plain fact is that this whole weight of argument has not been convincing. If anyone, anywhere, out of all these defenders of the faith, had succeeded in proving the existence of God, and even some meager outline of His nature, all men everywhere, upon a clear statement of the argument, would be persuaded by the proof. Yet unbelief is widespread. The case has not yet been made.

Many doubt that it ever can be made. They point to Kant's withering critique of the traditional arguments, in which Kant, as he himself put it, "had to remove knowledge, in order to make room for belief." [7] He showed that no clear evidence could be gathered from the world of experience and that however compelling our ideas of God, they do not carry with them the reality of God.

Thus when religion relies on reason for support it is making appeal to an uncertain court. At best it involves risks. A failure in logic, an unwary step, some wrong turning of the road, may lead to atheism. "Atheism may be said to live on the perils and failures of theism." [8] Here a bad defense is a betrayal. The actual record of apologetics is ground enough for this misgiving. Even so sympathetic a writer as the late Charles A. Bennett, speaking of the "vast accumulation of apologetic and philosophy of religion," in which religion justifies itself by reason, writes:

An impartial estimate of the success of these attempts leads one to conclude that they would better not have been made. Religion does not fare well under the assaults of criticism. [9]

It is not surprising, then, to find some contemporary theologians turning away from natural theology altogether. Karl
Barth, at the beginning of his Gifford Lectures, frankly owns
that he "is an avowed opponent of all natural theology." [10] He
reminds us that he is a teacher of the Reformed Theology, which
is the clear antithesis to that form of teaching which declares that man
himself possesses the capacity and the power to inform himself about
God, the world and man.[11]

Emil Brunner claims that the "apologetic attitude has characterized
the eras poor in faith," that "the hall-mark of logical inconsistency
clings to all genuine pronouncements of faith." [12] All these friends
of faith agree that it cannot make a logical case for itself. In this
judgment most of the foes of faith would eagerly concur.

2. Reason does not answer the persistent and deepest questions
of religion. All that reason gives you is a concept, the end product
of a syllogism, the implications of your own premises whatever
they may be, never the living God with all His majesty and mystery. Even if we could accept the traditional arguments for the
existence of God, and be persuaded by them, faith would not be
satisfied. To prove that there is an *ens realissimum* and to call that
God, tells us nothing about His nature or purpose. To prove that
God is the ground of all existence still leaves us only with a God
that is proportionate to the world of our experience. To accept
Him as the great Designer still leaves His purpose as ambiguous
as the intention we are able to discern in nature.

When we consider its actual performance in explaining religion,
reason disappoints us. Its final results are always too meager. It
sets up a religion within the limits of pure reason which is a pale
and formal moralism, a mere ghost of religion's self. It gives us a
dull, uninteresting truth. In all this men of faith feel cheated.
Reason, as Bergson said of the intellect, geometrizes—it has to distort in order to understand; it misses the living, awesome reality.

A theory is false if it is not interesting: a proposition that falls on the
mind so dully as to excite no enthusiasm has not attained the level of

truth; though the words be accurate, the import has leaked away from them, and the meaning is not conveyed.[13]

God as a sense of warmth about the heart, God as exultation, God as tears in the eyes, God as a rush of power or thought—that was all right. But God as truth, God as 2 plus 2 equals 4—that wasn't so clearly all right.[14]

Or sensitive souls speak through Unamuno:

So long as I pilgrimaged through the fields of reason in search of God, I could not find Him. . . . But as I sank deeper and deeper into the rational scepticism on the one hand and into heart's despair on the other, the hunger for God awoke within me, and the suffocation of spirit made me feel the want of God, and with the want of Him, His reality. . . . It is not, therefore, rational necessity, but vital anguish that impels us to believe in God.[15]

To the earnest believer of the present, to a person newly converted, or to a man who has just risen from evening prayer, the demand that faith give reasons must seem an impertinence, if not a blasphemy.

3. Faith demands the mystery of the unknown as the very condition of its life. It aspires to find a God whose ways and thoughts are higher than ours "as the heavens are higher than the earth." [16] But that which we know belongs to our domain where we are masters. We look down on what we have subdued through our knowledge. The impressive achievements of the scientific method, the rapid expanse of knowledge, and man's growing conquest over nature, contribute to his self-sufficiency. The challenge of faith nettles him. That there is a vast area of truth for which his reason is not at all sufficient, where he must falter, come to a dead stop, and cry out for the light as helplessly as an "infant crying in the night," [17] all this is offensive to the modern mind, which is fond of its rational mastery over nature. Yet this is the demand that faith makes upon reason. Richard Kroner writes:

The consciousness of the ultimacy of our ignorance is the source of religious awe. . . . Could we demonstrate or postulate the existence of God or an existing God by means of logical thought, this God would be our creature, an idol, and not the true and Living God who alone can fill us with awe. We cannot fear a demonstrated God; we cannot even love him.[18]

The mood of reason is confident self-assertion, that of faith is humility. Reason looks down on what it understands. Faith looks up to what passes understanding. Reason sees the universal range of its power. Faith sees the fragile nature of the thinker. Reason aspires to dwell in eternity. Faith is poignantly aware that it is a creature of time. Reason insists that everything in the world or out of it must meet its standard, conform to its demands, or be denied existence. This is the subtle self-deification of reason. Henceforth God is to answer my questions, conform to my judgment, prove and approve Himself to me. God then becomes my "problem." From this beginning modern man has ended by seeking to validate his own ideals, to pursue his own purposes, to establish the work of his own hands. For this human end God is regarded as an instrument.

Against this proud presumption of reason, whereby man aspires to a throne which he is not fit to occupy, faith rightly protests. God does not merely answer my questions; He puts searching questions to me. God is not to conform to my judgment; my true destiny is to conform to His. God is not compelled to prove and approve Himself to me; my question is, how may I be approved unto God? God is not so much a problem to me as I am to Him. My human ideals may require to be completely transvalued. My purposes may have to be thwarted and re-formed before they can really be fulfilled. I am neither wise enough nor strong enough to establish the work of my hands. God is not my instrument: I can find life only when I become His instrument.

So much for the case of faith against reason. These objections are implicit whenever faith refuses to accept reason as the final judge in matters of belief. If reason is to make any contribution to faith, it must take this case against itself into full account. But this is only one side of our dilemma. Reason has something to say to faith, to which faith must listen if it is to become articulate.

1. In its distrust of reason faith often goes to the opposite extreme of irrationality. It insists on the "ultimacy of our ignorance," which can mean only that God is beyond all meaning. Reason does not object when faith declares that our present categories of thought are limited to our experience; that the Object of faith is far beyond our experience, far above our thought; that from our present level the *Nescio, Nescio* of the mystics is the only appropriate human word about God; that the demand of reason that every reality pay tribute to its court is subject to the danger of pride; that provisional skepticism is the only road to truth. This is precisely the kind of critical work to which philosophy is devoted.

But faith keeps insisting on the actuality of God. What does this mean? It can only mean that He has a definite nature; that the lines are sharply drawn between what He is and what He is not; that in His being there can be no vagueness, no darkness, no internal contradiction; that, as the scholastics used to say, in Him essence and existence are one. What is this but the plain assertion that God is rational, at least to Himself? Therefore, that ultimate, as distinguished from provisional, skepticism is a denial of faith itself?

The exponents of faith sometimes glory in the irrational as such. *Credo quia absurdum.* They seem to believe that the defects of our human reason are inevitable and incurable; that theoretic interest is by its very nature hostile to the attitude of faith. When, therefore, such theologians insist on writing books in which they profess to despise reason and set forth their profession in pages and pages of reasoned argument, they are guilty of pretense. When these writers present conclusions which they insist belong to the realm of fact, meanwhile denying the ability of human thought to grasp what they say, they are in a very awkward position.

2. When faith tries to explain its meaning, it issues an invitation. It appeals to experience. It insists that its message is both relevant and urgent. It is factual: all men are under the judgment of God; all can find hope in His mercy. Yet while it invades the world of human meaning with its message, it denies the pertinence of the world of meaning which it enters.

This discontinuity of faith and reason, if followed, will lead straight to the pernicious conception of a two-fold truth. Brunner sees this danger when he refuses to admit that reason and faith are external to each other. This

could only mean a relation of irreconcilable opposition, the duality of truth which, however, if taken seriously would mean nothing less than the collapse of truth, for dual truth amounts to no truth at all.[19]

The world has had its sorry experience with this two-fold truth. It was implicit in some medieval thought, although it seems impossible to identify the source of the theory. A proposition could be true in philosophy and false in theology, or *vice versa*. This was designed to relieve the embarrassment of theology at the growing tension between itself and philosophy. But it had one unexpected result: it also freed philosophy from the domination of theology and prepared the way for the emerging independence of thought in the Renaissance. The best of the medieval minds, Albertus Magnus and Thomas Aquinas, recognized the danger of the two-fold truth and valiantly strove to reconcile philosophy and theology. But later thinkers widened the gulf between them.

The distinction is still implicit in much modern thinking. It has meant all but Christianity's complete surrender of the field of philosophy to secular thinking. The two-fold truth means a two-fold world, the separation of the world of secular affairs from the sovereignty of God. It is a poor bargain, this truce which the Church is often willing to conclude with science on the one hand, and with business and the State on the other. It leads by a short and direct route to the complete irrelevance of Christian faith. Men have not been slow to draw this conclusion. Yet precisely this inference becomes inevitable if the dualism between faith and reason is allowed to stand.

Such are the claims and counter-claims of faith and reason. They must be weighed carefully if faith is to become articulate and if reason is to be an aid to faith. But what do these claims mean? Is there any reconciliation? Must faith and reason continue their warfare or are they necessary allies in a common quest? The reconciliation is never to be brought about by compromise, by obscuring the sharp diversity of their interests for the sake of an uneasy peace. Reconciliation is rather to be sought in understanding the source and the nature of the conflict. This means a close study of the dual nature of man as thinker: man whose thought claims universal scope and validity, but whose perspective is finite, that is, conditioned by his relative position in history and in society.

On the one hand, thought is universal in intention. The human mind is never content to deal with any object or any event in isolation, as a complete novelty. Always it classifies: this experience is like that one. Always it seeks to relate one event to another in terms of regular sequence and of causation: this event seems to depend on that. Every advance in knowledge consists in relating objects and events to a larger context. Thought is systemic.[20] To deal with any event in complete isolation is to thwart intelligence. Once thought sets out to relate events and to discover common qualities, it cannot rest until it reaches some universal. Thought cannot grovel. It sweeps the skies and ranges through all time. There is a grandeur in the simplest logical steps of even an ignorant and foolish man, for by them he rises above the accidents of his birth and station and partakes of the eternal. There is a timelessness in all truth. However partial and limited my perspective, if I conceive any proposition as true, it does not occur to me that its truth was born with my particular insight. If what I grasp as true became true with my thinking and will lose its truth when I cease to think, I lose respect for it and no longer regard it as true. Partial glimpses of truth, these are usually the best that man can manage. Insofar as they are partial they have not yet attained full truth. But insofar as they are true they clearly appeal to something above and beyond the accidents of our own thinking. What have time and change to do with the truths of mathematics? Even when we disparage our transient insights, we are appealing to a standard that transcends our limitations in time.

In a similar way reason appeals to the consent of all thinkers. It cannot thrive in solitude. There is nothing private in truth; it is beyond and above my seeing it. When a scientist by experiment makes a new discovery, he eagerly awaits the confirmation of other scientists and their criticism of his conclusions. If I once suspect that what I regard as true is only my private notion, it is reduced to the status of opinion. When I learn that other people doubt my convictions, are unimpressed by my conclusions, cannot verify my observations, I, too, must share their doubt. In the daily clash of opinions, whether over scientific or economic or religious questions, the conflict has meaning just because all sides are implicitly appealing to what *ought* to be true for all observers, to what is above all private opinion. If men did not regard truth as universal, there would be no clash of opinions. Truth is public.

Insofar as I apprehend the truth, I have found something which is true for all time and everywhere and for all rational minds—this is assumed even by men when they try to deny it. When men write books trying to prove that truth is relative to the individual, or to a people who speak the same language, or to a culture, they are insisting that *this* truth at least is not relative. They are appealing to universal consent, that is, to the non-relativity of their truth, just as every serious writer on any subject tries to do. As Augustine saw, no significant doubt can even be formulated without an appeal to a truth that will clarify the doubt. If your doubt has meaning, it already implies a truth. You doubt that yonder tree is 100 feet high and thereby imply that the tree has a definite height, measurable in "feet." You doubt that the physician has correctly diagnosed the cause of this strange disease. Your doubt means that there is a real cause as yet unknown. You wonder if you really understand the inner purpose of a friend. You mean that he has a definite purpose which you may have missed. When a member of the family dies you may doubt that he lives after death. Your doubt is a senseless one unless you mean that there is a definite answer to your question.

By his thought, man is thus able to rise above his finite limitations of space and time. It is this power that enables him to know the structure of the stars even more certainly than he understands the workings of his own mind. It is this power which early Christian thinkers identified as the *imago Dei* and which Stoic thinkers called the divine element in man. Augustine in his *De Libero Arbitrio* held that vision and hearing were more excellent than the other senses just because they were more directly subject to social confirmation.

Seven and three are ten, and not only now, but always; nor have seven and three in any way at any time not been ten. I have said, therefore, that this incorruptible truth of number is common to me and any one at all who reasons.[21]

Man aspires to the universal. This is one side of the dual nature of man as thinker.

But the other side is just as evident. Man the thinker is finite, subject to all the limitations of his particular perspective. He was born in such a house in such a year, grew up as a child of these particular parents, received just this education, married this particular woman, had these children, enjoyed these successes, suffered these failures. He is a fragile creature, a child of nature and subject to its whimsical powers. He is never sure of his life and the specter of death always follows him. His anxiety over his insecure position leads him to assert himself, and to try as best he may to make his own life secure. This brings him into conflict with others who are also anxious by reason of their insecurity. He is a prisoner of his own fears and of his own thoughts. He is lonely.

He is bound by what has been called the "illusion of selfishness." Try as he will he can never know what it feels like to be another, his wife, his neighbor, his child. Always he is inclined to regard the fears, the sorrows, the triumphs, the delights, the hurts and the hopes of his neighbor as less important than his own. He sees life through his own eyes.

He is a member, too, of his own race and never quite shares the feeling of a man of another color. He is a member of a particular nation, feels the security of its power, or the lack of it, and can never quite understand why people of other nations do not respect the virtues of his own. He belongs to a social class and the anxieties of the members of another class are never quite real to him, no matter how sympathetic he tries to be. He belongs to a certain religious sect and can never quite succeed in suppressing the virtuous feeling of condescension when he consents to be tolerant of people with a different faith. He is also a creature of this earth and, as Mr. Einstein has reminded us, that fact has prejudiced even his geometry. Even more important, he was born in a definite year, that is, he is subject to all the limitations of his place in time. Here he is apt to attribute limitation only to those who lived in times past, since he studies them in history. It seldom occurs to him that his day will soon take its place with the past and be regarded only as a problem in historical study. The present arouses an inevitable snobbery.

However learned a thinker, he is still a creature whose perspective is finite. These limits introduce an inevitable bias into his thinking, mean that however he aspires to the universal, his approach to truth is relative to his own limited position and to his own personal interests. We are not Olympian gods dispassionately viewing all time and all existence. We are human beings with dozens of life and death interests, involved in a world of struggling desires and of painful decisions. We ought in all honesty to accept the fact of our finite limitations, to acknowledge them, and in so doing we shall in a measure be freed from them. But only in a measure, for it is the limitations of just this finite perspective that we are seeking to surmount and we never completely escape them. We are bound to exaggerate the importance of our private interests. Nor do we see how our finite and partial perspective obscures our objective truth which claims universal validity.

It is this dual nature of man which gives rise to the conflict of faith with reason. More specifically, it is when men become preoccupied with one of these two aspects of human thought that they are in conflict with men who are preoccupied with the other aspect. Until we bring these two sides of human thought into close relation, we shall not be ready to effect any reconciliation between faith and reason, or to resolve the dilemma of faith. We are really probing the fuller meaning of faith's dilemma when we honestly confront man's capacity for the universal in close relation to his finite perspective. What happens when men neglect one or the other of these two aspects of human thought? Fortunately, the history of modern thought will furnish us ample illustrations.

Some of the greatest philosophers have claimed a strange finality for their systems. Descartes, Kant, Hegel and Comte are fair examples. All human knowledge suffers from an "ideological" taint. Yet this is never mere ignorance of ignorance.

It always involves, besides, a conscious or subconscious effort to obscure a known or partly known taint of interest. . . . Hegel not only proclaimed the finality of his own thought but regarded his contemporary Prussian military state as the culmination of human history. Comte believed his philosophy to be final not only as a philosophy but as a religion; and with pathetic national pride he predicted that Paris would be the centre of the new universal culture which he would found.[22]

Theologians are by no means guiltless. Persuaded that they, at least, comprehend the subtleties of human pride, that they rely wholly on the Word of God, they do not see how the relativities of their own place in history, of their own class, race, nation, and denomination, have taken refuge under their theological systems and have thus been covertly given the secure eminence of God's truth. "Master, . . . we forbade him, because he does not follow with us." [23] Again, this is not purely ignorance of ignorance, but a "conscious or subconscious effort to obscure a known or partly known taint of interest." [24] Religious thinkers, too, have claimed a finality for their systems which in God's world they never could possess.

Indeed, there is good biblical and prophetic precedent for regarding the whole affliction of modern skepticism as a judgment of God upon the Church, Roman and Protestant alike, for its sinful pretension to finality. In the name of this claim it obscured its own finite and human perspective and tried to enslave the minds of men. It has a sorry record. It has been jealous of the freedom of the modern mind. It has shown little enthusiasm for the scientific method. It has had little sympathy for free inquiry and experiment, and would have stopped them to the great injury of humanity, had it possessed the power to do so. Authority was in danger. Now the modern mind, in revolt against the false authority of the Church, has turned against the faith of the Church as well, and has consequently fostered a skepticism which in turn threatens even the life of the Church.

Other men have been so impressed by the finite limitations of man as thinker, that they have been led to deny altogether the claim to universality. The whole skeptical, relativistic tradition in modern philosophy is an illustration of this tendency. David Hume was the outstanding and in some respects the most honest of all the empiricists. He insisted that all thought about matters of fact begins with impressions (sensations). It can therefore have no more validity than the impressions. When we see cause producing effect, we do not receive any impression of the transfer of causal power. Therefore, cause is reduced to mere sequence in time. Hume turned the critical method upon the self. If to be is to be experienced, then the self cannot exist since I have no impression of myself. "I never can catch *myself* at any time without a perception, and never can observe anything but the perception." [25] Hume did not stop to examine the "I" that was to do the "catching" or the "observing." As another has said, Hume went out of his house, looked in the window, and did not find himself at home. In consequence Hume reduced reality to the stream of the subject's conscious states and thus carried the empirical method to its complete skepticism.

The positivists, the pragmatists, the psychologists, have carried on this skepticism, by tracing the lowly origins of all our thinking. Yet they conceive their writings as being somehow above these limitations. The very fact that they write books and give lectures illustrates how inevitable is the appeal to the universal in all thought.

The Marxists, having pointed out the ideological taint in all bourgeois culture (and for this humanity owes them a profound debt), blandly assume that the proletarians are free from all such taint. This has led to the pernicious belief that there is no truth above their own interests and that scientific, historical, economic, political, and religious truths are whatever the party line declares them to be. This is a vivid example of what happens when any human society makes an absolute of itself, which falls within the biblical definition of idolatry.

It is clear, then, that we need to recognize both the capacity for universals and the limitations of our finite perspective, for both are essential elements of man as thinker. Unfortunately, there is no simple rule of thumb whereby we can detect the vitiating influence of private perspective upon thought. This is a moral, and ultimately a religious question, and we shall return to it. For the present the frank recognition of this dualism in man enables us to see in what direction a reconciliation between faith and reason may be found. For reason aspires to the universal, while faith is deeply involved with the finite and creaturely limitations of man.

CHAPTER 2

The External and Internal
Aspects of Knowledge

Man is at once a finite creature, subject to the limitations of his particular location in time and society, and at the same time capable of reaching after general truth that far transcends his finite location. These two aspects of man as thinker belong together. By analyzing them further we propose to attempt a reconciliation between faith and reason. If we are not fully successful, we can at least show that faith and reason must walk hand in hand, that they inevitably fail when they try to go their separate ways.

Man is a biological creature. Much of his thinking is frankly instrumental to his organic needs and revolves about such questions as what shall I eat and wherewithal shall I be clothed? It seems likely that the first thoughts of man were aroused by a thwarting of some biological need. Had all adjustments been painless and complete, it is doubtful that man would ever have thought at all. At this point the pragmatists are surely right. It is likely that a little child begins his thinking in difficulty and pain. We think best when we are forced to think. A felt difficulty presents itself as a problem. We are driven to find a solution. Thinking is clearly a serving of practical interests, at least in origin.

Many of our ideas are plainly instrumental. Our ideas of sword, hammer, pen, saucepan, motor car, road map, and compass all carry the suggestion of how we may use them. It seems likely that any idea we ever have, even of such abstract matters as the multiplication table, the laws of thermodynamics, Einstein's unified field theory, all are affected by the response we propose to make to them. In this sense Charles Peirce was surely right when he first pointed out that an idea is a plan of action. We never receive an idea in helpless passivity. Always the mind is active. It has no idea without a purpose being fulfilled in that idea. Thinking is an activity in which our interests play a lively part. Any thought, however general and impersonal, is our own doing, always involves our own purposes. A thought is therefore a deed.

Every idea has a practical aspect in that it answers to a subjective interest and so reflects our finite perspective. This was the insight of the pragmatists. Every idea has also a theoretical aspect, refers to the world outside ourselves. This aspect the pragmatists tended to neglect. The practical, interesting aspect Josiah Royce used to call the "internal meaning" of an idea. He gave the name "external meaning" to the theoretical aspect of an idea.

It is interesting to note that few philosophers or theologians have paid serious attention to Royce's distinction,[1] though it is central to the problem of knowledge and to the knowledge of God in particular. We need to pay careful heed to it, for out of it will come whatever insights we are to gain into the conflict between faith and reason, and whatever hope we may have for their reconciliation. We are indebted to Royce for the basic insight, although he would probably reject some of the applications we shall make of it, as he would certainly repudiate some of the conclusions we shall draw from it.

At every instant of our adult waking life hundreds of vague and disorganized impressions are pressing for recognition at the threshold of consciousness. We see only a few objects in the field of vision; we hear only one or two of the sounds of a given moment; we feel only a small part of the bodily sensations available at any time; we notice only a few of the people we pass on a crowded city street. What we see, hear and feel at any time is usually the result of our voluntary attention. Where we direct our attention reflects our purpose, our "internal meaning." Especially when we are actively at work by far the larger part of our attention is voluntary, purposive. In the case of the rhythm of a watch or a steam engine, it is possible to hear an added emphasis upon any one of four beats. Which beat receives the emphasis depends entirely upon our attention. Purpose limits attention to an epoch in history, an experiment in chemistry, a character in fiction, a musical theme, a contemporary political event, a screen door to be repaired, the weeds in the garden, the neighbor's dog.

Even when we refer to unyielding outward fact "internal meaning" is at work. I may be standing on the shore counting a group of sailing boats. I start the count. No matter what my internal meaning may be, out there are the boats, definite in number before I ever start counting them. The truth or falsity of my idea depends upon whether or not my idea conforms to outward fact. For I cannot spin outward fact from internal meaning.

But outer fact is not so independent of my internal meaning as it at first seems to be. For no outer fact can determine the truth of my idea unless I intend that particular fact. It is internal meaning that first declares, "*That* is my object; to *that* group of sailing boats I am referring. I wish to count *them*." If I say, "There are eight boats in that group," and you, looking farther down the water at another group reply, "Why, man, there are fifteen or more boats in that group," you are not judging the truth of my idea.

But the purposive activity of the mind is not exhausted in selective attention. Out of this chaotic raw material of sensation we build our world of experience. We see a distant church spire. What we see is only a tiny image. We interpolate, interpret, recognize; we allow for distance; we imagine the other side, the church beneath it, and the hidden structure of the spire. At any given moment the senses supply us with only a small part of what we think in the world of objects about us. The classical empiricists, Locke, Berkeley and Hume, were clearly wrong in reporting that the mind is passive in perception.

In the sensations of the present moment we are interpreting in terms of past experience. We easily deceive ourselves at this point. We have at the moment a perception of scarlet. Surely we have nothing to do with the particular character of that scarlet except to see it! But in order to recognize it as a particular shade of scarlet we have to call upon our whole past experience of colors. It is impossible, for example, for any of us to recover our first experience of scarlet, as an infant. It is likely that the first color distinctions which a baby recognizes are between light and dark objects. What colors we ever see depend upon our past experience. Wives are usually much more sensitive to color variations than their husbands and find it hard to be patient with male ineptness. All our sensations are highly sophisticated. The simple ideas of Locke turn out to be very complex. A colleague from the physics department reports once being suddenly aware of the floor shaking beneath his feet. He thinks this feeling, before he recognized that he was in an earthquake, was probably the nearest to a "raw" sensation that he ever experienced in adult life. But these patterns through which we refer to past experience for our meaning are in part the creation of internal meaning.

The world of our experience is much more than a conglomeration of sensations. We are constantly referring our sensations to the outer world. This, too, is an activity of the mind to which Mr. Santayana has given the name of "animal faith." We have to fit our sensations into that outer world. We must find both unity and diversity in that world. It is hard to see how we could have unity without diversity, or diversity without some unity. We employ "categories" of thought, systems of order, and seek to discover laws. These laws not merely serve to "explain" larger areas of fact, but are reflections of our own purpose as well. Perhaps the basic interest of all scientific minds is the discovery of uniformity. Einstein's unified field theory is hailed as significant because it seems to bring into one complex formula such diverse phenomena as the radiation of light, electro-magnetism, chemical valence, and gravitation. This "bias" toward unity is a reflection of human internal meaning, as indeed are all the cate-

gories of human thought. Thought is an activity and therefore
implies a product. The world of our experience is in some sense,
then, the product of our own purpose. As soon as we recognize
this activity of the mind,

just so soon do all the old comparisons of the mind to a wax tablet,
to a sheet of paper, or to other like passive subjects of impression lose
for us their meaning. Mental life becomes for us, in view of these facts,
a field of constant activity.[2]

Knowledge involves not merely the logical relation of outer
fact, but the variety of interests that find expression in these facts.
The finite perspective of the knower is embodied in these interests. All attempts to persuade people of the truth of an idea,
all marshalling of evidence, all statements of logical implication,
are at the same time appeals to the purposes of our auditors that
need fulfilling. If we cannot win the sympathetic consent of another's purpose, no argument will ever prove compelling. No
one is ever convinced against his will. His will may change
grudgingly, but until it is modified he accepts no new truths.

At this stage of our argument the impatient realist is ready
to rush upon us in anger. "This is mere quibbling," he will say,
"and the plain truth is that the outer world goes on its way largely
indifferent to this 'purpose' of yours. It grants you at best a few
years to live and think and pass your futile judgments upon a
world that in the end will extinguish you and your 'internal
meaning.'" The world is not such as we would like it to be; it
thwarts and finally defeats all our purposes. As Royce himself
put the case:

Chaos or order, joy or defeat, tears of despair and shouts of victory,
mysteries, storms, north winds, wars, the wreck of hearts, the might of
evil, the meteors that wander in interplanetary darkness, the suns that
waste their radiant energy in the chill depths of lifeless space,—these
are all facts,[3]

and facts regardless of what your fragile pulse of internal meaning
may happen to be.

Yet such facts as those just cited are never merely external. Even such facts would have no meaning apart from our own purpose. They exercise compulsion over us partly because we coöperate in our own compulsion.

The disappointed lover is such, not merely because his mistress rejects him, but because he wills to love her. If he did not so will, she could not reject him, and would lose her "compelling" character altogether. She controls his will by his own connivance. . . . What we experience is, in one aspect, always *our own will to be compelled by facts.*[4]

We should note carefully that the world of outward, compelling fact is not merely the world of wind and climate, but the world of mind as well. Indeed, the most fateful compulsions of our day are those that come from the minds of men. The very destiny of the world is even now being shaped in human thinking. Because of these hard and "compelling" mental facts millions may die and life on this planet be turned into a curse. Literature is full of stubborn fact in the world of thought. The king in Hamlet, struggling to be free of his conscience, is living in a world of unyielding fact.

> "What then? What rests?
> Try what repentance can: what can it not?
> Yet what can it, when one can not repent?
> O wretched state! O bosom black as death!
> O limed soul, that struggling to be free
> Art more engaged!"[5]

The world of our own will, created by our own internal meaning, may be the world of fact that thwarts us. In one of his earliest unpublished writings Royce pictures the fate of the incurable individualist. He

comes into the world with a desperate desire to make it subservient to his ends. By hard treatment, by toil and bruises, and bloodshed and tears, he learns by and by that there are some things he cannot accomplish, some barriers he cannot break down, some enemies he cannot subdue, some aims that can never be realized. In his narrow circle he learns to live, if the task be not all too hard for him; and then discontented, groaning, hoping for better times, complaining of mythical lost happiness, cursing his lot and any of his fellows he may think more fortunate than himself, he wears the gloomy days away till the last sigh escapes him and men put him out of sight and forget him.[6]

But let us look more closely at what the angry realist is saying. He is telling us that the world is what it is and that we ought to recognize it as such. It is clear that one thing is worrying him: the havoc wrought in the long history of human thought by "wishful thinking." Men have held the most fantastic beliefs for long ages because they wanted to believe them. They have resisted the advances of science because new conclusions were painful, compelled them to the hard labor of rethinking their world. Even today what hoary prejudices block the way to new truth and imprison men in the darkness of error! This emphasis on internal meaning is really a covert encouragement to a romantic view of the world, where each remakes the world of fact to suit his fancy. We ought rather to combine our efforts to root internal meaning out of our thinking once for all and to adopt the fine impersonality of the scientist. Such will be the angry protest of our realistic friend.

But is the scientist impersonal? There is a widespread notion, sometimes fostered by men of science, that a man can enter his laboratory, divest himself of every subjective interest, and sit passively before his apparatus while the objective truth forms itself in his otherwise empty mind. This picture is pleasant enough, as most illusions are, but quite out of touch with the realities. The plain truth is that nature maintains a stony silence before such a vacant mind. Nature never answers any questions until they are put. To learn to ask the right question is the method of good science. If you want to see the subjective interest, the internal meaning, of the scientist, look at the form of his questions. Or better still, study the structure of his apparatus for his crucial experiment. Most important scientific results, we are told, come these days in the form of mathematical equations, pointer readings, or photographic plates. No blank mind can make any sense of them. It requires a well informed body of internal meaning to make these readings.

Nature often answers the scientist's questions with a "No," but her negatives are seldom brutal. Usually they carry hints of a sounder hypothesis, a better form of the question. Disinterested knowledge, then, is a contradiction in terms. Even the most abstract mathematical thinking is guided by subjective interests; otherwise research might consist in counting the pebbles in the ballast of a mile of railway track. To approach an object of study by laying aside all subjective interest is simply not to approach the object.

It is highly important to recognize this principle in the social studies. A historian without any internal meaning, without some personal interests, would be helpless. He could not even make a start in his work. He might sit down before all the census reports ever compiled in this country, or in all the civilized nations of the world. But what would he do with them? But give him an interest, even a prejudice, a thesis to prove, and he can at least make a beginning. A "biased" historian is better than a completely "objective" historian, simply because an objective historian cannot be a historian at all. Of course, it is important that his "bias" be generous, held in full awareness and with humility, and subject to the best canons of historical criticism. As William James once put it:

If you want an absolute duffer in an investigation, you must, after all, take the man who has no interest whatever in its results: he is the warranted incapable, the positive fool. The most useful investigator, because the most sensitive observer, is always he whose eager interest in one side of the question is balanced by an equally keen nervousness lest he become deceived.[7]

But we return to our angry realist and mark more closely what he is saying. He is telling us that we ought to take a certain attitude toward the world of outer fact. He is using the language

of ethics: he is appealing to a higher internal meaning! Here he
is on solid ground. For it is utterly vain to attempt to dispel internal meaning. That would mean the destruction of all thought.
But internal meaning, being a form of activity, is subject to moral
judgment and correction. The range of moral quality in internal
meaning is vast: all the way from the most benighted sinner who
allows his meanest prejudices to govern his thoughts, and who
is not disturbed about it, to the saint who moves with fine humility
and persistence in the clear light of growing truth. When we seek
to win young students to the scientific attitude, we are not asking
them to renounce all attitudes! Growth in knowledge is on its
inner side a process of purification of purpose. The correction
of the judgment is at the same time an ethical clarification of
internal meaning.

Indeed, the central puzzle of knowledge is to decide what
questions to ask, what purposes have a right to be fulfilled. This
is true in every field of inquiry. It is also true in religion. What
are man's most worthy purposes? Why do I ask questions? What
questions are most urgent? What is the chief end of man? These
questions are implicit in every inquiry into the meaning and
truth of religion. A man has a responsibility for his creed, and
his beliefs depend upon the kind of man that he is.

Another ethical interest of immense importance is here at stake.
The pose of impersonality which the modern mind often assumes
is a serious pretense. This pretense has bad results even in the
realm of abstract scientific thought. But as we move into those
realms of thought where personal and vital interests are involved,
the pretense has more serious consequences. It is one thing to be
indifferent about a metaphysical theory. But it is quite another
thing to be indifferent when that theory involves my very existence and my destiny. It is quite easy to be impartial in listening
to an argument in court over a fine point in law. But when a
prisoner's life depends on the decision of just this technicality,
you could hardly expect him to follow the argument with de-

tachment. It is one thing to maintain scientific objectivity in the statistics of some economic study. But when the study involves one's own financial future, it is much harder to retain scientific objectivity. The danger lies in the pretense. It is the pretense of the scientist that he can be impersonal when he undertakes, exceeding the limits of his science, to pass judgment upon God. It is the pretense of the social "scientist" who looks forward to the day when he may claim as much exactness and objectivity as the natural scientist. It is this pretense that has obscured the partial and relative character of all philosophical and theological knowledge. It is the pretense of any man who fancies that he can enter a controversy over economic or social issues, free from the bias of his own position in society. It is this pretense, ignoring the ideological taint of class, race, and position in history, which gives rise to the sinful pride of reason.

The way toward truth lies in the frank recognition of these pretenses of disinterestedness. As long as our subjective interests are unrecognized, we shall be deceived by them. But if we can bring them to light, if we are honest enough to confront them, we shall in a measure be able to discount them and so be freed from their deceit. When two men are engaged in a controversy involving rival economic interests, they can never come to agreement as long as each maintains that he is unbiased in the discussion. But if each can be led to see what his personal interests are, and more important, to recognize the personal interests of the other, there is hope of common understanding. This is one of the most urgent issues of our day, especially in the fields of social, economic, and political controversy, where pretense is open and unashamed.

If objectivity means the suppression of subjective interest, it is an impossible ideal. But what is the actual working use of the term "objective?" It refers to social corroboration. As we shall see more fully in chapter 6, we never regard a truth as established until it has been confirmed by independent observers. The truly objective is that which is open to a consensus in contrast with that which is essentially private and unavailable for social checking.[8] The problem of knowledge, seen in this light, is a problem of reconciling our purposes with those of other observers. It is an ethical problem: how to live with other people.

As a further illustration of the importance of internal meaning in all knowledge, we turn now to one of the persistent questions of technical philosophy. This problem also throws light on the question of how we may come to a knowledge of God. Non-philosophical readers may regard this problem as artificial. But it has concerned many of the best minds in the history of western thought. It is the question, how do we come to a knowledge of individuals? For knowledge as external meaning has to do with universals and can never quite reach the individual. That we have to do with individuals seems certain. But how do we know them? Of course, there is a quick and ready answer: all our knowledge begins with individual facts and out of individual facts we construct our abstract ideas and general laws. A child begins by knowing individual persons and things. This is true, but he does not begin by knowing them *as* individuals. There is every evidence that the child knows these individuals in terms of their common qualities,

their recognizable, and, for that very reason, abstractly universal features. . . . A child's early vagueness in applying names, his "calling of all men and women fathers and mothers," as Aristotle already observed, shows that our primary consciousness is of the vaguely universal.[9]

This character of knowledge is implicit in our language, in our use of common nouns and verbs. We can never convey meaning except in terms of universals.

This means that while the individual is unique I can never know that which is unique about him, for I must know him only in terms of qualities which he shares with other beings. The difficulty becomes most acute in our knowledge of God. For God is by definition individual and unique in an absolute sense. There is no other like Him. To apply any predicate to God is to imply that in this respect, He is equal to other beings with which He shares this common quality. If we apply any human symbol to God, such as personality, Father, Judge, Savior, Friend, we are reducing Him to human proportions, missing precisely that which is unique and individual in Him. It was this difficulty which led the prophet, speaking on behalf of God, to ask, "To whom then will ye liken me, that I should be equal to him?" [10] As we have seen, the mystics answer by denying that any predicate can be attributed to God. God, they say, can be known only by the negative path. Of God you can say with truth only, "He is not that," "He is not that." God is not to be captured within any human symbol, however pure and high it may be, much less within the concepts drawn from our earth-bound experience.

But we encounter the same difficulty in our knowledge of other persons. For the human individual is likewise a unique being. I may compare my friend with others who are like him, contrast him with these same men, but I have not reached that which is unique in my friend. I am still describing him in universal terms. Royce went so far as to say [11] that I never know my own father, simply because I must know him in terms that could be applied to many other fathers. The same difficulty appears in our knowledge of physical objects. F. H. Bradley said [12] that even judgments that purport to be individual are universal. When I say, "This road leads to London," I have not yet defined that which is unique about this road, for the same thing can be said of many other roads. Try as hard as you will, as long as you deal only with external meanings you cannot get beneath the universal to the individual.

Aristotle—and his doctrine survives in modern Neo-Thomism— held that that which individuates any being is its substance, a material substance in a physical object, a spiritual substance in a spiritual being. But thus to define the individual is to put him forever beyond the reach of our knowledge, since the substance which is beneath all observable qualities is unknown and unknowable. Aristotle recognized this and agreed that the utmost that could be won in the knowledge of an individual is the "*infima species*." The idealists (Hegel, Bosanquet, Bradley, and to an extent Royce followed them) have said that there can be only one unique individual, the Absolute. All finite beings are unique only in a derived sense, only by reason of their having a definite place within the Absolute. But as finite beings we plainly cannot see an individual from the point of view of the Absolute. Therefore, the individual is as much beyond our knowledge as ever.

What shall we say? Our knowledge is of universals and the individual is unique. The difficulty remains insoluble as long as we sunder external from internal meaning. For individuality is borrowed from the finite perspective of the knower; it is a function of internal meaning. Of course, we know our fathers, but we know them in terms of internal meaning, of our relations to our fathers, not merely in abstract, general terms. The judgment, "This road leads to London," is universal in form and must remain so in its external meaning. But said to a prisoner who is on his way to London to stand trial for his life, it is an intensely individual judgment. It then becomes his road to doom or freedom.

Royce argues that love is the supreme principle of individuation. He illustrates by the sorrow of a child whose toy soldier has been broken. He will not be comforted by any substitute. You may buy him an identical soldier from the same counter, or a better one with a fancier uniform. But it is for the broken soldier that he longs. His exclusive passion for the toy soldier is what makes of that soldier an individual.

This practical, this passionate, this loving, this at first thoughtless dogma of love, "*There shall be no other*," is, I insist, the basis of what later becomes the individuating principle for knowledge.[13]

The more deeply a human individual is loved the more of an individual he is. We are made selves in part by the range and quality of the love others bestow upon us. Supremely, we become individuals because of the unique and individuating love of God.

Here Royce was in much closer *rapport* with biblical thought than are the Neo-Thomists with their Aristotelian principle of individuation.

Our knowledge of individuals is thus existential in character. Nor can we become individuals apart from a comprehensive purpose. The natural man can scarcely be called an individual. His many purposes are at warfare with each other and he is really a multitude. He is not born a self. He may become one. His becoming an individual depends upon the comprehensiveness and the significance of the ideal around which he centers his otherwise disunited and scattered life.

It is devoting the self to a cause that, after all, first makes it a rational and unified self, instead of what the life of too many a man remains,—namely, a cauldron of seething and bubbling efforts to be somebody, a cauldron which boils dry when life ends.[14]

Your self is your total reaction to your world, the gathering of your fragmentary interests into one comprehensive loyalty. This, your internal meaning, combined with the internal meaning of other persons, makes you a real individual.

We can never know other individuals as persons, nor can we become persons ourselves apart from internal meaning, the purposes that reflect our finite position in history and in society. This is the clearest answer to be made to a contemporary philosophical school that is trying to reduce all meaning to objective, symbolic language. Ordinary language, they hold, is too full of ambiguity to be exact. It carries emotional overtones that distort its meaning. With the hope for semantic clarity every lover of truth must find himself in complete sympathy.

But this same school dismisses ultimate questions as having no meaning, simply because they are incapable of scientific verification or disproof. The questions themselves are nonsense and the answers attempted, just so much verbal magic. Just here the dangerous pretense of ignoring internal meaning comes into sharp focus. For if they assume that meaning can be completely depersonalized in purely objective symbols, they end by having a mere skeleton of knowledge. If they do acknowledge their own purpose, then they are clearly guilty of dogmatism. What they then say boils down to this, "Our needs for semantic accuracy, our internal meaning to seek only clarification of external meaning, form the only valid cognitive purpose a human being may hold. Your meanings that you attempt to find in clarifying man's relation to God are not proper meanings at all."

In all this it becomes clear that faith is essential to knowledge. Faith has always invited disaster whenever it posed as a substitute for knowledge. And those who scoff at faith in the interest of knowledge need to see how constantly they make use of faith. Faith is essential even in the exact sciences. We have seen that we can have no knowledge of an object apart from some hint as to how we propose to respond to that object. But when we move from the world of impersonal objects to our knowledge of persons, faith assumes a much more important place. As we shall see later, the character of our response to other persons determines whether we are to know them or not. In the same way our knowledge of God is conditioned by the response we propose to make to Him. But the affirmative response of man to God is Christian faith. Faith thus becomes the highest form of internal meaning. Alike in the world of science and in the quest of divine truth, there can be no knowledge without faith. They are inseparable.

Just this difficult analysis puts within our reach certain preliminary gains which we should now claim. You will recall that one of the objections of the disciples of faith was that knowledge gives only an abstract truth about God, never the living God. This has led some defenders of the faith to despise knowledge and to cling to faith. In the light of our recently gained insight we may now say it is quite true that knowledge of itself gives us only an abstract truth. We now know why—because it is sundered from internal meaning. But when faith claims to dispense with knowledge, when it despises the theoretic interest as hostile to faith, it lays itself open to the dangers of superstition.

Again, faith has protested against the pride of position which is fostered by the power of reason, saying that we tend to despise what we know as that which we have mastered; that the "consciousness of the ultimacy of our ignorance is the source of religious awe." [15] If this is true, faith ought to dread knowledge of any sort, and from whatever source, even from revelation. It should eagerly foster ignorance as the basic condition of "religious awe," on the ground that the less our knowledge the stronger our faith. But it should now be clear that pride of opinion is a response to knowledge, and as such belongs to the internal meaning of ideas, not at all to their external meaning. Thought itself, so far as its external meaning is concerned, is neither proud nor humble. The cure of pride of opinion is not blind ignorance, but purifying faith. Faith has nothing to fear from knowledge. On the contrary, it is its nature to seek knowledge with eagerness.

Indeed, it is the man of little knowledge who struts, displays his opinions, and pretends to know all the answers. Eminent scholars and scientists are usually men of remarkable humility. It is when I am ignorant of one of God's noblemen that I can fancy myself his equal. But when I understand him, I recognize that "it was but unity of place that made me dream I rank'd with him." [16] Any New Englander, whose forefathers were men of the sea, and in whom the family tradition lives, will tell you that men who know the sea respect it. It is the novice who takes foolish chances. Then shall we say that as our knowledge of God grows we shall lose our awe of Him? I think not.

CHAPTER 3

The Limits of Reason

We have seen that faith accompanies knowledge of any sort. The mind is active in all knowing. All ideas are in part plans of action. The impersonal, detached observer is a figment of fancy. Not among men will you find this privileged spectator. Internal meaning is itself a reflection of our finite perspective, our limited purposes.

But this analysis leaves us with a sobering problem on our hands, to which we have already paid some attention in chapter 1. Since all thought is an activity of a "biased" observer, however noble and generous his bias, are we not driven to the relativity of all truth? Consider what we have found. Each observer is conditioned not only by his own experience, but by the history of his own culture. His categories of thought, however impersonal, still reflect the bias of that culture. To be sure, we believe that our interests are capable of refinement. We do learn from experience. The growth of knowledge consists in part in testing our purposes, in finding the right questions to ask. Thus the growth of science is marked by its discarding old, humanistic, emotionally-laden symbols, for impersonal, emotionally-neutral symbols. Indeed, its advance can be measured by the progressive depersonalizing of its categories. But these more adequate symbols are still the work of the human mind. They are selected by internal meaning as more appropriate to the task of knowing. Are we not then back with Protagoras, the Sophist, saying that all truth is relative to the observer? What warrant have we for believing that our ideas, reflecting as they do our finite perspective, ever encompass the real to which they refer? Whether we look at a distant mountain, or study a problem in physics, or try to understand the rise and fall of an ancient Egyptian dynasty, or think of God, aren't we driven in all honesty to say, "This is how it appears to me"? Can we ever say, "This is the truth as it really is"?

Let us take the example of the distant mountain. As I watch the lights and shadows play upon it, there five miles to the west, I am plainly seeing it from a perspective. It would look different from its opposite side, or from the air, or from its foot. But whoever sees yonder mountain must see it from some perspective. And in spite of his perspective, there is a measure of truth in what he sees. He is surely not looking at his own idea of the mountain. Perhaps we need all perspectives in order to understand the mountain.

But is there any favored perspective? Is my position favored simply because for several days I have seen it from the east? The man who lives five miles on the other side of the mountain will hardly concede that my perspective is better than his. Is it best seen from the air, thus relating it to other nearby mountains? But mountains are notoriously flattened when seen from above. Is the artist who paints it the favored observer? Or the lumberman who puts a price on its timber? Or the real-estate salesman who raises the price of nearby land because of the magnificent view? Or the climber who seeks the best way to the top? Or the geologist who can tell you its history?

Who is the favored observer of God? How shall we seek Him? By what symbols is He to be known? What are the worthy purposes that will be honored by success in our quest? What is the quality of faith that will apprehend Him? What are the limits of our reason in knowing God, limits that are inherent in our status as human, culturally-conditioned beings? These now become our central questions.

Men of unbelief will quickly say that all this talk about faith beclouds the issue. Granted that some internal meaning is essential to all thought, this merely means that each observer occupies a relative position. We still must seek useful symbols and the most fruitful are the symbols of exact science. It is semantically unsound to talk about God. But to approach our world with the workable symbols of science is to bring the world increasingly under the control of man. Let logical analysis point the way.

Men of belief will also protest our use of faith. After all, they will urge, knowledge is warranted belief. Seek the rational evidence. Leave faith just now to the more intimate and personal moments of religious experience. Make all due allowance for the relative position of the knower. Does not the weight of rational probability lie on the side of God's existence? If this evidence can be established, does it not mean that we can come at least to a partial knowledge of God, thereby laying a stronger foundation for faith? Can it be that the Creator has left no signs of Himself in His workmanship?

Can we by ascending bring God down to our human comprehension? Are there limits beyond which reason cannot take us in our knowledge of God? Can we be sure that these limits will not be surmounted in the future? Or is there an inherent absurdity in arguing from our earth-bound concepts to the God who is above all our thinking? Barth has recently written of "the humor and the fragility" of the traditional proofs.

We cannot answer these questions without referring to Kant. We shall, therefore, review his criticism of the theistic arguments, seeking to reappraise the arguments in the light of his criticism, and, if possible, to find the limits of reason in man's attempt to discover God. Here I must entreat the patience of some readers, for whom this Kantian criticism seems like old straw from which the last grain has long since been threshed. But it is not so. While an impressive succession of thinkers have assumed that Kant did destroy the rational grounds for belief in God, the last word is far from being said about the theistic arguments, or about Kant's criticism of them, or about the critics of his criticism. His treatment of the evidence for the existence of God is so basic, that any appraisal of the rational approach to God must take his work into account.

1. The Ontological Argument

The ontological argument, as formulated by Anselm in his *Proslogium*, is based upon an implied relation of thought to reality. That, whose non-existence involves contradiction, necessarily exists. As Anselm puts the argument, even a fool has in the understanding an idea of something than which a greater cannot be conceived. But if this greatest possible being exists in the understanding alone, it is not one than which a greater cannot be conceived, since to exist in the understanding and in reality would be greater. Since the non-existence of this greatest of all beings involves contradiction, God necessarily exists. This is Anselm's argument.

What art thou, then, Lord God, than whom nothing greater can be conceived? But what art thou, except that which, as the highest of all beings, alone exists through itself, and creates all other things from nothing?

Whatever thou art, thou art through nothing else than thyself. Therefore, thou art the very life whereby thou livest; and the wisdom wherewith thou art wise; and the very goodness whereby thou art good to the righteous and the wicked; and so of other like attributes.[1]

What does Anselm mean by "great?" Plainly the whole argument turns on this point. As developed most fully in the *Monologium* he means unconditioned Being, that which owes its existence to nothing else, which is therefore timeless and eternal. For if it came into being it would owe its existence to another. And if it ceased to be, that which caused its destruction would be greater.

Put in this form the argument is clear. Its origin goes back through Plato to Parmenides, who first enunciated the principle that necessity of thought implied necessity of being. "For it is the same thing that can be thought and that can be." [2] Thought also requires that that which *is* be eternal, immutable, indivisible. So for Anselm there must be some unconditioned being that exists in its own right. In our experience we encounter many conditioned objects, contingent in that they come into being and pass away. They are therefore not ultimate since they depend on something else. To this something else I refer, or beyond that until I come to that which is. That there is such a being is a requirement of all thought. Without it nothing could exist. This self-existent being is what I mean by God. This is the heart of Anselm's argument. As Hocking has described this argument, it "reasons that because the world is not, God is." [3]

Gaunilo, a contemporary monk, made the obvious reply to Anselm's argument. I may have an idea of the lost island, surpassing in excellence even the Islands of the Blest. Since it is more excellent "not to be in the understanding alone, but to exist both in the understanding and in reality, for this reason it must exist." [4] Surely, Gaunilo continues, no one can be expected to take such an argument seriously. To this Anselm replies that if Gaunilo can adapt the argument to any being except unconditioned being, that than which a greater cannot be conceived, "I will give him his lost island, not to be lost again." [5]

Kant's criticism was directed against Descartes' adaptation of Anselm's proof. Descartes had said:

I clearly see that existence can no more be separated from the essence of God than can its having its three angles equal to two right angles be separated from the essence of a (rectilinear) triangle. [6]

But there is a difference. The judgment about the triangle, as Kant showed, is analytic. The judgment about God is synthetic. In the one case I am simply analyzing the nature of a triangle. In the other I am going from concept to existence.

To accept a triangle and yet to reject its three angles is contradictory, but there is no contradiction at all in admitting the non-existence of the triangle and of its three angles. The same applies to the concept of an absolutely necessary Being. Remove its existence, and you remove the thing itself, with all its predicates, so that a contradiction becomes impossible. [7]

Kant suggests that you may make analytic judgments about God with confident certainty. The proposition "God is Almighty" is true analytically. The most perfect Being cannot be conceived as suffering from any limitations of His power. But it does not follow that God exists. Reason cannot supply that synthetic judgment.

Kant's most devastating critique of religious knowledge appears in his section on "The Antinomies of Pure Reason." Here Kant showed that when reason seeks to go beyond the realm of possible experience in search of ultimates, then seeks to apply these ultimates to the world of experience, inevitable contradictions follow. The whole weight of his criticism of the ontological argument is gathered into one sentence, "Now the unconditioned necessity of judgments is not the same thing as an absolute necessity of things." [8]

This last sentence is the crux of the argument. It involves the central question of the relation of thought to reality. If the necessities of thought are *in any way* related to the necessities of being, then the ontological argument holds. It can be refuted only on the basis of the whole critical philosophy of Kant and the skeptical conclusions that he draws. If you are any kind of a realist in your theory of knowledge, assuming as you then will that thought must conform to the real, you are driven to assume some ultimate or ultimates. If you do not come to underived being, that which owes its existence to nothing else, you come at least to some semi-ultimate such as space-time, the electron, the whole process of nature, etc. The decision to stop short of underived being must always seem arbitrary. The resolution will soon be broken. If you do not resume your search, if you are content to rest and not look farther, someone after you will refuse your resting place and press on. This search for the ultimate, this curious thirst of the human mind for the beyond, has led men to all the discoveries of theoretical science and is the soul of his philosophy. He is not likely to give up that search. "I have an idea of a most perfect Being," said Anselm, thereby confessing himself a man. Fateful idea! condemning the human spirit to restless search, endless inquiry, persistent journeyings, until it find rest—in God Himself? Anselm's understanding of the human mind is profound. Let him who is weary of seeking, rest with his demi-god, his finite ultimate. Humanity will pass him by.

As for the idealists who hold that thought is determinative of reality, beginning with Hegel, they refused to accept Kant's criticism. Thus F. H. Bradley:

Since Reality *is* qualified by thought, it therefore *must* possess whatever feature thought's essence involves. And the principle underlying these arguments—that, given one side of a connected whole, you can go from this to the other sides—is surely irrefragable.[9]

Whatever your theory of knowledge, realistic, idealistic, or skeptical, there can be no question about the intention, that is, the internal meaning, of all thought. It is realistic. Only in moments of idle dreaming is the mind content to watch the play of its own ideas. Whenever the serious work of life and thought must be resumed, it dismisses these "ideas" as "mere fancies." It will not consent to suffocate within the walls of its own subjectivity. As Bosanquet put it, the presumed subject of every judgment is the real. Every judgment, however casual, implies the preface, "Reality is such that . . . " If I say, "All S is P," I mean, "Reality is such that all S is P." The same principle applies to hypothetical judgments. When I say, "If wishes were horses then beggars would ride," I do not mean to imply that there ever has been or will be a time when wishes will be horses. What I intend to say is, "Reality is such that, if wishes were horses then beggars would ride."

You cannot disparage thought except by thought. When a materialist tells us that the human mind is nothing but a by-product of physical causes, he does not see what that does to his own argument. When a psychologist calmly announces that he has been thinking, and the conclusion of his thinking is that there is no such thing as thinking, he does not usually see the grim humor of his position.

The only creature that can prove anything cannot prove its own insignificance without depriving the proof of any proof-value. Any radical depreciation of man involves an equally radical depreciation of the scientific thinking which supplies the supposed evidence.[10]

Thought must proceed on the assumption that it is capable of qualifying the real world.

Thus when Mr. Dewey declares that thought is a function of the biological organism, he plainly makes an exception of his own statement. Mr. Dewey is a serious man and means to be taken seriously. What he intends is plain: "Reality is such that all thought is a function of the biological organism." When the Marxists say that all systems of thought, including the most abstract mathematics and the most speculative metaphysics, are "ideologies," they obviously intend to make an exception of their own statement. In this one case, at any rate, they succeed in getting beyond "ideology" to reality. If they are in earnest, and the Marxists never seem frivolous, what they mean is, "Reality is such that, etc." When the Freudians assure us that all our ideas of ultimate things are but symbols created out of subconscious need, they plainly do not mean to apply this to their own statement. If they are in earnest what they mean is, "Reality is such that, etc." When the theologian tells us that reason is so corrupted by sin that it cannot make a right judgment about anything ultimate, he cannot bring this particular judgment of his under that indictment. Theologians are the most serious of men and they plainly intend that here, at least, their thought is a successful qualification of the real.

This serious intention of all thought, this purpose to qualify the real, is the standing reply to such symbolic interpretations of religion as that of Mr. Santayana. These studies of symbolism may contribute to our understanding of the religious process within us. But to accept them as substitutes for the religious Object is, to put it bluntly, a cruel kind of trifling with the most important concerns of the human spirit. Now all this is involved in the ontological argument. Thus Mr. Hocking:

It is this point that the ontological argument aims to put into our possession; the reflection which this argument embodies is the only, and wholly simple, defence against our besetting subjectivity.[11]

A second, and kindred, implication of all our thinking is contained in the ontological argument: not only does idea aim at the real, but the real is in some way amenable to idea. That the ultimate is rational and akin to thought is a premise with which all thought must begin. Philosophy must proceed on the assumption that the world has meaning and that this meaning is not finally inaccessible to the mind of man. In a more modest way all science also lives on the same assumption. Nature will answer questions when they are rightly put. Call this a belief if you will, without it no scientist would so much as enter a laboratory or begin an experiment. Mr. Hocking is dogmatic at this point.

There is no inaccessible truth. If any object has possible bearing on human interests, such as to make it matter of choice, it has a bearing on human fact also—there is some cognitive way to it.[12]

We should be cautious about drawing facile conclusions from this basic assumption of all thought. From our belief that the ultimate is rational it does not follow:

(1) that the ultimate consists of ideas. That conclusion has often been drawn, but it does not follow from these premises.[13]

(2) That my ideas determine the nature of reality. This can be affirmed only on the basis of an idealistic identity between my partial ideas and the completed ideas of the Absolute.

(3) That it yields one specific empirical fact, or that any theory can claim from it more than partial confirmation. Our reasoned explanations have continually to be revised by the sudden appearance of seemingly irrational fact.

(4) That reason is the only or principal quality of our human nature. Plainly, it is neither. Preoccupation produced the rationalists. In fact we often behave irrationally. Feeling colors judgment; our finite perspective and group prejudices give pretentious finality to our opinions. Habit and custom determine most of our con-

duct; critical questions seldom disturb our practical doings. To some folk they come—apparently never.

But it does follow that the ultimate is not irrational or paradoxical. Grant that human knowledge has all the limitations you wish to impose on it, that it is applicable only to the world of sense experience, or that it is determined entirely by practical ends, that it is governed by the needs of the organism in adjusting to its environment, or that it is corrupted by sin, still the ultimate is rational. Implicit in all serious talk, whether it be of science, philosophy, economics, politics, theology, is the belief that the world's meaning is deeply related to man's idea. Once we have entered a discussion, honesty and reason, as well as courtesy, demand that we respect what is implicit in all talk.

It follows that paradox has a limited, though very useful, value. There can be no self-contradiction in the ultimate. When reason uses paradox, as in dialectical theology, she recognizes that she is in an area of profound ignorance, that here her hitherto useful categories are helpless. She has a lively feeling that the paradox has meaning, that here she is "getting warm." Significant paradox is a sign which reads: "Stop! Reflect! Humble yourself! Important area! New and momentous insights to be discovered!" But God cannot be irrational. In Him there can be neither darkness of meaning nor shadow of irrationality. Even Karl Barth, who certainly cannot be accused of encouraging any rational approach to God, writes, "Christian faith is not irrational, not anti-rational, not supra-rational, but rational in the proper sense." [14] When Barth goes on to say that Christian faith is able to stand up to the simple question of its truth, he implies at least this much of the ontological argument, that the real is the true.

This belief that the real is *en rapport* with the ideal is plainly no proof. But it is a working belief, so central in all thought, so much a part of ourselves, that to deny it would mean the death of all thought. And while we must observe our own caution about facile conclusions drawn from this belief, it is only honest to say that this assumption of the rationality of the real does give weight to a spiritual rather than a naturalistic interpretation of the world.[15]

How far, then, does the ontological argument take us? As proof it fails for the simple reason that such proof would have to stand outside our experience, yet include our experience along with the real in one purview. Obviously such a proof is forever inaccessible to man. Further, if the proof were valid, what would it establish? The existence of an ultimate being or beings, rational in nature, *en rapport* with the reason of man. Such a conclusion would satisfy no religious faith, set no nerves tingling, arouse no devotion. But as a central belief, indispensable to all thought, a belief implicit in all speech, the ontological argument is valid. The most we can say is that this belief favors a spiritual and indeed a theistic interpretation of the real. Further, it is important to see, as Kant pointed out, that every conceivable argument for the existence of God rests back upon this argument; that if the necessities of thought carry no implication for the real world, then no theistic argument has any validity.

2. The Cosmological Argument

This argument, which was used by Thomas Aquinas, rests on the principle of causation. A cause is necessary to explain any contingent being. If that cause is contingent then it must in turn be the effect of a prior cause, and so on until you come to necessary being. But as the analyses of modern science and philosophy make clear, causation is much more a demand of thought than a *direct* inference from natural events; and we are back with the question as to whether or not a necessity of thought carries with it necessity of being. The cosmological argument therefore turns out to be a disguised form of the ontological argument and stands or falls with it.

In any event the causal argument is the least significant of the three. At best it only proves a cause proportional to the world. And if God is proportional *only* to this world, we may just as well work with this world as we find it. God as cause of this world adds nothing. As Mr. Hocking has expressed it:

Historically men have lifted their minds to God rather because the world is unsatisfactory, than because it satisfies. We wish a God who is greater than the world, also better than the world as found, and also more real.[16]

3. The Teleological Argument

Kant approached the teleological argument with respect.

It is the oldest, the clearest, and most in conformity with human reason. It gives life to the study of nature, deriving its own existence from it, and thus constantly acquiring new vigour.[17]

This is the familiar argument from design. There are many evidences of a wisdom at work in the world, beneficial complexities that could not "just happen." These marks of a wise design argue a "sublime and wise cause," whose unity "may be inferred with certainty from the unity of the reciprocal relations of the parts of the world." [18]

But the argument fails in two important respects. (1) It might prove the "contingency of the form, but not of the matter" of the world. The most that could be established by such a proof would be "an *architect of the world*, always very much hampered by the quality of the material with which he has to work, not a *creator*, to whose idea everything is subject." [19] (2) The argument proves at most only a wisdom commensurate with the range and quality of the design which we happen to observe in the world. We can say only of such a cause "very great," "very wise," not that it is "all-great" or "all-wise." But this is plainly not enough. So the step is taken from partial to complete proof—how? By suddenly abandoning the empirical proof and "by means of transcendental concepts only," it infers the existence of an absolutely necessary Being. "Baffled in its own undertaking," it takes refuge in the cosmological proof, which is just the ontological proof in disguise.[20]

The writings of Darwin seemed to rob teleology of much of

its force. Many of the favorite evidences of design which were found in the human body, for example, are now seen to be the outcome of an age-long process of natural selection. Nature produces with a lavish and careless abundance. There is a consequent struggle for survival and those organisms which are better equipped survive, propagate their kind, and pass on their improvements to their descendants.

It has often been pointed out that to explain the emergence of complicated structures in animal organisms by the "law" of natural selection is wisdom after the fact. It explains little. It builds upon the fact of variations in each successive generation, when the fact of variation itself calls for explanation. As someone has said, "It does not help to explain why I am here, by telling how my uncles and aunts went away." The general belief among biologists that acquired characteristics are not inherited, forces the inquiry into microscopic changes within the germ plasm itself.

But when you take the long view of the evolutionary process, see the development from a one-celled organism with undifferentiated function, until you come to man, and especially to that aspect of man's nature which enables him to transcend nature and himself, with his ability to reflect, to feel the obligation of a moral imperative, to give up his life for another, to search out the mystery of the stars, to create his poems, his dramas, his paintings, his music, you are confronted with an amazing development indeed. To break up this problem into a vast number of minute variations, is to substitute for the large problem an almost infinite variety of small problems and to come no nearer to an answer. To say that this long process was self-contained, that unconscious matter could by however long a process and by however many minute stages work itself into self-consciousness—this is to talk nonsense, to surrender the principle of continuity, and to abandon all pretense of rational explanation. Or if we take the course of the newer naturalism and assume that the rich variety of the end was in some way implicitly contained in the beginning, then we are compelled to assume a richness of life in primitive matter for which we have no empirical evidence whatever. The more honest way is that of Conwy Lloyd Morgan and S. Alexander, who recognize frequent emergents in the evolutionary process which could not be predicted from the lower (or earlier) level. But this leaves the whole upward trend of evolution as a series of unexplained facts, which Alexander would have us accept with "natural piety." If we must choose—and as common men we must choose every day of our lives—between blind energy and the wisdom of God, is not God the much more reasonable choice?

Almost forty years ago Lawrence J. Henderson wrote a book on *The Fitness of the Environment*. He discovered a wide variety of conditions which are essential to the maintenance of life. In his study he confined himself to the physical and chemical properties of water, carbonic acid, and the numerous compounds of carbon, hydrogen and oxygen. He was dealing with biological life in general and did not take into account that side of man's nature which transcends nature. The wide variety of conditions which make animal and vegetable life possible makes interesting reading. Among the very many conditions which he points out we mention only a few. (1) Water is the most efficient of all known solvents. The solubility of various substances in water, without their being affected chemically, is basic to life. (2) The surface tension of water makes its presence in the soil possible. (3) The fact that it reaches its greatest density a few degrees *above* freezing, a fact without apparent explanation, prevents lakes and rivers from freezing from the bottom up. (4) The constant temperature of the ocean is due to the high specific heat of water. No other liquid could "bind" so much heat on evaporation, nor release so much heat on condensation. The amount of heat required to evaporate water from 100 square kilometers of tropical ocean is "vastly more than all the energy employed in the metabolism of the total population of the United States." [21] These last two facts have a vital effect on a climate favorable to life. When he considers the large

range of such facts, each of them essential to life, he concludes
that the fitness of the environment

results from characteristics which constitute a series of maxima—unique
or nearly unique properties of water, carbonic acid, the compounds of
carbon, hydrogen, and oxygen and the ocean—so numerous, so varied,
so nearly complete among all things which are concerned in the problem that together they form certainly the greatest possible fitness.[22]

To the man of faith this book contains many grounds for thanks-
giving to the Creator, though it has probably seldom occurred
to a worshiper to thank God for the high specific heat of water
or its efficiency as a solvent. But such "evidences" are of a purely
religious value. The man of science cannot use them. Henderson
goes on to claim that the variety of peculiar conditions necessary
to life on this or on any planet is so great that there is "not one
chance in countless millions of millions" that these conditions could
have existed by accident. Some explanation must be sought, but
it must be sought in terms of natural law. He sees little hope that
this explanation can be found in existing "hypotheses and laws."
Yet as a man of science he cannot admit a directing purpose.
"Science has finally put the old teleology to death."[23]

But the death sentence was premature. Clearly teleology is no
instrument of scientific research. Yet F. R. Tennant[24] has renewed
the case for the teleological argument in an impressive way. He
bases his case on five kinds of evidence. (1) The world conceivably might have been a chaos "in which similar events never
occurred, none recurred, universals had no place, relations no
fixity."[25] The fact that it is "more or less a cosmos" is a fact that
calls for explanation. (2) The "internal adaptedness" of organisms
does not admit of a mechanical explanation. Plants have no discernible psychic life, yet they behave as though seeking to fulfill
purpose. (3) The inorganic world is adapted to life by a wide
variety of complex and independent yet necessary connections,
as illustrated above by the study of Henderson. (4) Nature is
"saturated" with beauty, quite out of any discernible relation to

the fitness of the organism to survive in the struggle for existence. (5) Nature is the seeming parent of men with their moral life. Its uniformity and its impartiality are a pre-condition of moral life. When you consider these facts, not one by one, but in their connectedness, then "divine design is forcibly suggested." [26]

But to suggest forcibly is not to prove. Indeed, the teleological argument has provided a happy hunting ground for all kinds of theological novices. The common man who claims to find purpose often means that he has discovered his own private purpose. To the man of faith, who believes in God on other grounds, there is vast evidence of the goodness of God in nature, for which he should offer praise to the Creator. But let him hesitate before he pretends to read the purpose of God in nature. Let him ponder all the cruel aspects of nature which seem brutally indifferent to beauty, duty, or truth. Let him sit with a man whose wife and children have just been lost in a storm. Let him visit a Chinese village whose population has been wiped out by cholera. Let him consider the random variations of nature, as though she were testing out all sorts of tentative and half-formed ideas. Many of her ideas proved fantastic, as witness the fossil remains of long-extinct species. Within the species nature seems greedy for re-production, blindly, insatiably greedy, at any cost to the individual, with the result of brutal conflict for survival. She seems bent on nothing more from the individual than that he reproduce his kind. In short, nature seems to speak of purpose *and* of blind striving. It is no argument that we can prove God from the purpose of nature if we are unable to discover more than hints and fragments of purpose. As to whether these purposes are good, the answer of nature is ambiguous.

To return to Kant, having destroyed the possibility of a speculative theology, he reassures us that if we cannot prove the existence of God, by the same token we cannot disprove it either. For if we cannot exceed the limits of possible experience, the atheist is barred from certainty as well as the theist. If we can believe in

God on other grounds, our belief is safe against disproof. In this respect Kant was certain that he had rendered faith a substantial service.

Aside from the theistic arguments, are there other grounds for belief in God? Yes, said Kant, and they are to be found in the moral experience. The moral law has an unconditioned and an absolute character. It speaks to us not in counsels of prudence, but in the categorical imperative. It bids us do our duty, not from any private advantage we might gain thereby, but for duty's sake alone. The good will is governed only by respect for the moral law.

The *summum bonum* is the proportionate union of happiness with virtue. While duty must be done regardless of happiness, happiness should be coupled with virtue. Since this is obviously impossible in this life, there must be a future life in which virtue can be rewarded by happiness. Furthermore, the absolute commands of morality are such as not to be fulfilled in this life. They demand an immortality for their fulfillment. There must be a wise and good ruler of the universe to make this immortality possible. On these grounds Kant says, "I firmly believe in God." [27] The belief in God, freedom, and immortality must not be taken back into the world of speculative reason. They are "practical postulates," required *if* the moral law has validity. But they do not amount to theoretical proofs and Kant would have repudiated the attempt of later thinkers to base theoretical certainty on the moral life of man.

At first thought, we may pronounce Kant's emphasis upon the moral life, and the belief that the moral life justifies, as a perfect instance of internal meaning. Morality is the supreme practical interest of man and this is precisely what we have defined as the realm of internal meaning. In Kant, then, we have a clear instance of faith and reason working together. But closer inspection will prove this quick surmise to be wrong. For Kant's categorical imperative is a pale and formal account of internal meaning. It is only remotely related, if at all, to man's finite position in time, history, and society, and it ignores the determining part played by these vital interests in both thought and morals. It is this neglect of vital interests that gave to Kant's moral theory the abstract and formal character of which his critics have often complained.

This neglect of the full wealth of internal meaning is also responsible for the abstract and formal character of his treatment of such theological doctrines as original sin and redemption in his *Religion within the Limits of Pure Reason*. When Kant went on to develop his "faith" it was a pure moralism that he produced. He denied divine grace, saying that if any divine help comes to us we could not recognize it, nor understand the manner of its operation. We must therefore confine ourselves to the effort to deserve the assistance of divine grace. But a deserved grace is no grace at all. Forgiveness, Kant goes on to argue, consists in replacing the old man of impure motive with the really new man of pure motive. In other words, no man is forgiven until he deserves forgiveness, which again is a contradiction in terms. Kant had revolted from his pietist background and its enthusiasm and he had no use for *Schwaermerei*. He said that a man ought to be ashamed to be found on his knees in prayer. It is said of him that if a guest at his table remained standing to say grace, Kant would tell him to sit down!

In any event Kant is not seeking to establish the existence of the God of the Bible. As for the "wise and good ruler" argument, it has never carried much weight. The idea of the *summum bonum*, if it is self-evident as Kant maintains, is really a form of the ontological argument which Kant used in his ethics after having discarded it in his speculative theology. Kant's distinction between the speculative and practical uses of pure reason is formal. The moment you begin to "postulate" the existence of God in the interest of morality, you are talking about an existence which belongs in the field of the speculative reason. Thus even Kant's practical assurance is caught in the destruction of his speculative theology.

To sum up, what are the limits of reason in its search for God? (1) We have no mathematical proof for the existence of God. The unbeliever can always make a case for his position, as indeed he has often done. (2) The ontological argument was found to be the basic argument. It amounts to the belief that thought intends reality as its object and that the real is in some sense rational. (3) The evidences of design in nature are ambiguous. On the one hand, the upward course of evolution makes a directing purpose a much more rational assumption than a non-purposive mechanism. On the other hand, it is impossible to read the purpose of nature with any certainty. (4) The demands of morality are significant enough to merit an important place in our total comprehension of the world. But to sever moral certainty from theoretical certainty is not to establish the fact of God, even for faith. (5) Granted the most that can be said for the arguments, they do not lead us to the God of the Bible; nor does the God of the arguments expose the promethean character of our self-assertion, reveal any love that will heal our uneasy conscience, nor give us any confidence that our deepest needs have an answer in the resources of God. It would be rash to conclude, as some theologians have done, that the day of natural theology is over. Men of later generations will continue to study these arguments. Nor can the sober man of faith of our own time dispense with them. It is one thing for reason, apart from faith, to seek to reach God through the traditional arguments. But it is quite another thing, as we shall see in a later chapter, for the man of faith to relate his faith to the world of experience. He may find in the connected and combined force of these arguments a higher degree of probability and certainty than he can find as a basis for any other vital decision. But our enthusiasm for reason must be humbled by the apparent inability of reason, working in isolation from faith, to establish any significant certainties for faith.

CHAPTER 4

The Experience Philosophy

Near the close of his book, *The Varieties of Religious Experience*, William James called for a new science of religion. He had already illustrated the method of the new science. It was to be based on a study of religious experience. In his book James had drawn largely on the unusual, even the abnormal, because they provided the most vivid illustrations. Such a science, James now proposed, could discover that which is common and dependable in all religious experience. It could develop hypotheses, testing them positively and negatively as any hypotheses are tested. It could reduce the number of such hypotheses, eliminating the more objectionable. It could test its findings by comparison with the findings of other sciences. It could mediate between different faiths. It could discriminate "the common and essential from the individual and local elements" [1] in religious beliefs. James hoped that such a science could "eventually command as general a public adhesion as is commanded by a physical science." [2]

He was willing to state his own preliminary conclusions for the new science. They can be briefly put. The common element in all religions is in two parts: an uneasiness and its solution. "The uneasiness, reduced to its simplest terms, in a sense that there is *something wrong about us* as we naturally stand. The solution is a sense that *we are saved from the wrongness* by making proper connection with the higher powers." [3]

This poses an interesting question. If we want a Christian knowledge of God, why not study the experiences of those who believe in Him, see what God has done in and for them, drain off what is clearly of subjective origin, or individual "over-belief," and by making a scientific study of the remainder, come to a clear knowledge of God through an understanding of what He does? The modern temper, wary of the *a priori* inferences of reason, impressed by the substantial results achieved by the empirical method, will find this a congenial approach.

At any rate James' suggestion was quickly accepted. In the years that followed there appeared a large number of psychologies of religion, each of which sought to achieve a scientific knowledge of religious experience. Insofar as these are accurate descriptions, they contain much that is of immense value for Christian education. But a serious ambiguity inheres in this appeal to experience. Are we to study our subjective experiences as such? Then we should be fatally preoccupied with internal meaning, the world of our own desires and fancies. Or are we to consider the "higher powers" through observing what changes they make in our experience? Only in the latter case would the new approach be really scientific. For preoccupation with the private, the subjective, is the very denial of the scientific method, which is throughout a quest for public, socially-verifiable truth. This ambiguity may be observed in James' statement quoted above. But if we could study the religious Object through an analysis of our own experience, we might come to a dependable knowledge of God.

Long before James wrote, men had begun the study of religious experience. It appeared in the theology of Albrecht Ritschl and his followers. Denied access to the real God by Kant's critical philosophy, Christian thinkers now turned to a study of human values, and especially of moral values. Since that time theology and philosophy of religion have been full of talk about values. While these were the highest values known to man, in themselves worthy of great respect, they were still human values. More than one philosopher has been burdened to prove the "objectivity of values," that in these values he was touching the reality of God Himself. In the meantime God's chief business was supposed to be the conserving of these human values. Thus G. B. Smith wrote,

"The religious life is the quest for the reinforcement of our highest ideals by the spiritual contribution from the environing universe." [4]

To all this the psychologists made a prompt and obvious reply. Religion is an escape; a compensation for the otherwise intolerable position of man. Psychology simply took Christian theology's evaluation of its own field and said, "Very well, if that is religion, it belongs to us and we shall show you what your religion really means." If Christian theology is a study of man's subjective attitudes, such as his feeling of dependence, if your concern is with human values and ideals, we can show you the source of these meanings of yours. Religion is just a projection of human ideals upon an otherwise indifferent outer world. This kind of explanation of religious experience has lately been given the name of "psychologism." We are not here saying that its explanations are convincing, although they have much to teach the serious student of religion. The theory of "escape" is strangely inept when applied to Jesus praying in Gethsemane, "Father, all things are possible to thee; remove this cup from me; yet not what I will, but what thou wilt." [5] This was a confronting of the real, not an escape from it. Indeed, the explanations of psychologism break down whenever any man of faith listens to and obeys the Word of God.

One of the first and most influential thinkers to elaborate the projection theory of religion was Ludwig Feuerbach. He held that the Christian religion is really a study of man. What man worships in God is what he worships in himself. This is proved by the fact that the Christian God is most loved and adored because He is merciful toward man, makes the welfare of man His chief concern.

The divine being is the pure subjectivity of man, freed from all else, from everything objective, having relation only to itself, enjoying only itself, reverencing only itself—his most subjective, his inmost self. [6]

All the various attributes of God are just human attributes divested of their limitations. God as understanding is simply the human understanding, which deals with universals. God as a morally perfect Being is nothing else than "the moral nature of man posited as the absolute being." [7] The love of God is the very love by which man loves himself. Prayer is "the certainty that the power of the heart is greater than the power of nature, that the heart's need is absolute necessity, the Fate of the world." [8] Faith is the "infinite self-certainty of man, the undoubting certainty that his own subjective being is the objective, absolute being, the being of beings." [9] In its doctrine of immortality religion at last throws off its disguise. Here the man of religion openly avows what has been his secret, although basic concern all along—his own being. "If I am not immortal, God is not God; if there is no immortality, there is no God;—a conclusion already drawn by the apostle Paul." [10]

Not much can be said by psychologism that Feuerbach has not already said, except to fill in the details. Santayana sees poetry in religion, yet it corresponds to no reality. The proper question to ask of religion is not, is it true or false?—but, is it better or worse? Freud seeks to explain religion in terms of infantile sex impulses toward the mother and father. These impulses are not socially allowable, are repressed into the subconscious, and escape the "censor" only in dreams and under psychoanalysis. Men symbolically create the image of a god who is in some sense a father, and who, like his human prototype, is at once the object of our dependence and our dread. Adler attached great importance to feelings of inferiority as the source of our religion. Jung does admit the central therapeutic power of religious faith. Other popularizers of these three have freely used the principles of "projection" and "compensation" as the explanation of man's pathetic attempts to escape the intolerable limitations of his existence by phantasy thinking.

In general, those who regard religion as symbolic or psychological projection divide on the question of friendliness to religion. Feuerbach, Santayana, and Jung attach great importance to it.

The difficulty, however, is that they have "let the cat out of the bag." Men will take their symbols seriously only as long as they believe them to point to objective reality. But once the secret is out, once men believe that prayer is only auto-suggestion, they will soon give up the whole business as humbug. Faith will not trifle. It can endure only under the conviction that it points to genuine truth. The impulse is healthy. Indeed, the psychologists themselves insist that phantasies are dangerous, that mental health in part consists of looking at the real, naked and unadorned by pleasant illusions.

It has often been pointed out that any psychological explanation of the appearance and growth of religious experience does not touch the question of religious truth, any more than a study of learning affects the validity of scientific inferences. It is to confuse the psychological with the logical. Assume for the moment the truth of Christian belief, that God has created man with his very limitations, his fears, his insecurity, his restlessness, that he might find his salvation, his courage, his confidence, his rest in God alone. If that is true, then man may, yes must, exhibit those very compensations and projections which the psychologists have taken so many pains to explore.

A religion that is preoccupied with its own feelings, centered in its own needs, makes a poor showing indeed in contrast to science which has a healthy respect for fact, combined with a tough disregard of how I happen to feel about it. As another has put it:

The truly humble are those whom something has humbled. *Serenity* is a good thing, and if a man choose to secure it by mental calisthenics rather than by twenty grains of aspirin a day, that is his own business. But what one finds slightly ridiculous in the practitioners of the first kind is the notion that there is some moral or spiritual excellence about *their* serenity. For if all you want is to *feel* a certain way, what difference does it make whether you breathe deeply or take aspirin? Both are drugs; yet no one, so far as I know, has yet felt justified in becoming lyrical over the peace of aspirin that passeth all understanding.[11]

No clearer word has been spoken against the idolatry of subjectivism than by Josiah Royce.

Have a care lest what you reverence shall turn out to be your own vague and confused notions, and not the real divine Truth at all. Take heed lest your object of worship be only your own little pet infinite, that is sublime to you mainly because it is yours, and that is in truth about as divine and infinite as your hat.[12]

Recent empiricists have tried to escape the blight of subjectivism. But they insist that the Object that we encounter in religious experience is within the world of nature and accessible to scientific inquiry. In his book *A Common Faith*, John Dewey dissociates himself clearly from those who try to prove the existence of God by a study of experience. For one thing Dewey denies that there is any special religious experience and finds rather a religious quality possible in any experience. Further, experience yields no knowledge of any reality above or beyond the world of nature.

Dewey does not deny the reality of mystical or religious experience, but insists that the "revelations" of such experiences are inferences brought into those experiences from previous theories. He cites as evidence the same kinds of mystical experience that are variously interpreted in different cultures.

Dewey believes that all the values which have been attributed to religion can be achieved without belief in any supernatural Being. Indeed, he thinks that man will move more eagerly toward these ideal ends, when he surrenders belief in the Christian God. This does not mean that man spins the ideals out of his imagination, that they are "rootless ideals, fantasies, utopias." [13] They have their roots both in nature and in society. He complains that "militant atheism" has too often treated man in isolation and ignored the social origin of our ideals, while humanistic religion is "pale and thin . . . if it excludes our relation to nature." [14] Dewey pleads for the religious attitude as against the established religions. He adds that this attitude "needs the sense of a connection of man, in the way of both dependence and support, with the enveloping world that the imagination feels is a universe."[15] He proposes that the name God be given to "this *active* relation between ideal and actual." [16]

Henry Nelson Wieman in his recent book, *The Source of Human Good*, takes a position not far from that of Dewey. The "active relation" of Dewey becomes the "creative event" in Wieman. This event creates new goods for man and in man; creates, enriches and widens human community; enlarges meanings and remakes human ideals. Wieman writes with a much clearer appreciation of the inner meaning of Christian experience than does Dewey, who has the air of a novice when he writes about religion. Wieman recognizes six saving functions in the metaphysical (Christian) myth of supernaturalism.

It has directed the absolute commitment of faith away from all created good and thus delivered man from bondage to any relative value and has thus saved him from good become demonic. It has established a demand for righteousness far beyond the socially accepted standards of a given time and place and so has broken down the arrogance of the "good people" and opened the gates of forgiveness to each and all, since the difference between better men and worse men is slight compared to the extent that all have fallen short of the transcendental demand. It has established a bond between men vastly deeper and more important than personal affection or kinship, mutual interest or shared ideal, institution or race. Moreover, it has shown evil to be deeper and darker than any wrong done to society, to any group, or to any person, because in the last analysis evil is against the transcendental reality. It has revealed an obligation laid upon man which overrides any obligation derived from society, tradition, ideal, or loyalty to persons. Finally, it has opened possibilities of creative transformation beyond anything that could be expected from human effort, idealism, or any other such power.[17]

No greater service can be imagined. . . . We shall try to show that creative good . . . is, in fact, the actual reality which has done the work and played the part fictitiously attributed in the Christian tradition to something eternal (nontemporal), immaterial, and superhistorical.[18]

Wieman thus agrees with Dewey in rejecting any God who is above or beyond the world of nature. For both men the scientific method is our only road to verifiable truth. New methods of "inquiry and reflection have become for the educated man today the final arbiter of all questions of fact, existence, and intellectual assent." [19] For these men and all whom they represent the method of scientific empiricism excludes belief in the biblical God.

D. C. Macintosh has made the most thorough attempt of all these writers to construct a Christian theology out of a scientific study of religious experience. The basic data upon which the science of religion is to be built are the values of the true, the good, and the beautiful, in both individual and social life. These values are called divine because they are worthy of our utmost allegiance and devotion. In this sense they are absolute, and it is reasonable to think that they will always be so for all human beings.

Whence do these values come to man? From a variety of processes, among which is to be apprehended a divine factor which we may call God. This factor is not to be "exclusively identified" with human individuals or the social aggregate. But Macintosh does not distinguish between the part of "the divine factor" and that which human beings and human society contribute to the growth of ideals. Thus a basic muddiness vitiates the proposed science from the start, that is, if we are to look to the new science for any reliable knowledge about God. Nevertheless, Macintosh is certain that the values exist, and that the divine factor has been at work in them. The divine factor not only fosters human ideals, it causes human personality itself "to emerge" and educates "humanity toward the knowledge, appreciation and choice of permanently valid values." [20] With God's work thus defined, "it may be affirmed as a known fact that God exists." [21] Our source of scientific information about God is then the process, which is called divine, and which produces persons and educates them in values.

God as the "divine-value-producing factor in the universe" [22] works on condition of the "right religious adjustment" on the part of man. This "right religious adjustment" includes concentrated attention on spiritual and moral ends and upon God, surrender of self to God, faith to appropriate His help, "active response to the appeal of the moral ideal under the inspiration of this faith," [23] and wholehearted persistence until the desired result is attained. This adjustment includes for sinful man "the change of will called repentance." [24] God does take the initiative. The "value-producing factor and behavior in the universe" does not wait for man's right religious adjustment to appear, but seeks to produce this adjustment in man, even against his opposition, forcing man "to the method of trial and error, or self-correction and success." [25]

So much for preliminary statement of method. Macintosh now proceeds to formulate thirteen empirical laws on the basis of available evidence. In order not to prejudice the case, the word "god" does not appear in these laws. The expression "divinely functioning reality" is substituted. I quote the first two:

1. The elemental law of empirical theology (law of the answer to prayer). A divinely functioning reality, on condition of the right religious adjustment for a specific volitional effect (the promotion of the good will) tends to produce a desirable change in that direction in the will and character of the individual concerned, and this may be regarded as the basic, dependable "answer to prayer."

2. The law of a definite beginning of a normal and normative ethico-religious life (law of conversion or regeneration). On condition of the right religious adjustment being made sufficiently comprehensive for the volitional effect to cover the principles and activities of the whole life, divinely functioning reality tends to bring about the moral regeneration of the individual, as the comprehensive answer to his comprehensive prayer.[26]

Other laws cover such experiences as perseverance, growth, repentance, peace of mind, joy, love, assurance, divine guidance, social salvation.

On the ground that we know objects from what they do, it is

claimed that through this empirical science of religion we can "know a good deal about God." [27]

Reviewing then the laws of empirical theology, and making the transition from laws to theory in the usual scientific fashion, we may say that the Divine Reality is a reality that dependably responds to the right religious adjustment, that answers true prayer, that regenerates the human spirit, that maintains the regenerate life, that promotes the health of the spiritual life and develops essentially Christian ethico-religious character. Furthermore, this same Divine Reality convicts of sin, gives peace and joy, and "sheds abroad the love of God" in human hearts. Religious assurance and moral guidance are also among the gifts of this Reality which the early Christians called the Holy Spirit. And what is thus done for the individual on condition of the right religious adjustment is also done for the church and would be done for the community or for the world on the same condition.[28]

This is, indeed, a sizable body of knowledge about what God does. But as yet we know little about the nature of God. We know only "a divinely functioning reality." We do not know that God is one. We know only that reality includes a divine power. This is all that is claimed for a science of religion. Macintosh now proceeds to construct a "normative theology," beyond the limits of empirical evidence, on the basis of "imaginal intuition" and faith. The elements of this theology must have three characteristics: (1) they must carry subjective assurance; (2) they can contain nothing which is in contradiction to the findings of religious experience; and (3) they should be reasonable at least to the extent of being incapable of disproof. In the findings of the science of religion Macintosh claims to have a norm by which he can test and measure all the claims of faith. The God of faith must be consistent with the God who is revealed in experience. On this level of theology Macintosh seeks to conserve "to the utmost 'whatsoever things are true' in the theology which has functioned vitally in the traditional, evangelical Christian faith." [29] He also has regard for "moral optimism." The contents of this faith are what we must believe if we are to live as we ought. We have a moral right to this belief.

What, then, must we believe, in order to live as we ought? What, in brief, are the contents of this theology? God is one, personal, purposive, conscious, intelligent, active. Whatever be the extent of His wisdom and His power, so far as His character is concerned he is worthy of complete trust and love. In contrast to the moral perfection of God as Judge, sinful man stands condemned. There is a way of deliverance from sin that does not deprive man of his freedom. There is endless existence for all who will make good use of it.

So much of a normative theology is possible for a man who doubts the historicity of Jesus Christ. Macintosh believes in the historical Jesus, as the beginning of the Christian Church would otherwise be a hopeless historical enigma. Moreover, there is immense psychological advantage in the historical Jesus. He is "the highest individual embodiment in history of those absolute values or spiritual ideals which we have designated as divine." [30] His uniqueness is the result not merely of the divine initiative, since that is "impartially bestowed" (upon all men, Macintosh seems to say), "but to the dependable divine response to the right religious adjustment which we may well believe was habitual with him." [31] In other words, the uniqueness of Jesus was in the unique perfection of his "adjustment" to the divine initiative. This it is which makes him the supreme revelation of God, the Son of God and Savior of men. However, all revelation in and through another, even that through Jesus, is "second hand." The most important and saving revelation of God for anyone is His revelation in the life and experience of that individual himself. Clearly experience is the only valid revelation for Macintosh. The only authority which Macintosh will recognize is the expert "who has intuited and thought out and tested and verified the truth for himself." [32]

The normative theology goes this far. This still leaves untouched the question of the extent of the knowledge and the power of God. Is He great enough for our trust? Jesus so believed, yet his belief was not fully verified in his life. This belief is common to all men of faith. Yet it is not a verified knowledge. It is a

theoretical possibility, a not yet discredited intuition, a faith which may possibly stand up under all legitimate tests of its probable truth, as being still a reasonably permissible as well as a practically valuable faith.[33]

But this testing of the highest claims of faith belongs to the third level of knowledge, that of metaphysical theology. Into this doubtful domain Macintosh does not go. He merely points the way. Here we must be willing to pass from the assurance of faith, through tentativeness, to a hoped-for objective certainty. He hopes that metaphysics can give both a "more reasonably defensible content" as well as "a more rational certainty" to theology.[34] Yet on every one of the basic issues of metaphysics which Macintosh lists in his last chapter, the philosophers themselves are hopelessly divided. It is indeed a forlorn hope that theology can expect from metaphysics either a rational purification of content or a more rational and, therefore, a greater certainty than it now has. For to which of the metaphysicians shall we turn? It requires no great imagination to picture the sudden and embarrassed modesty with which most of them would decline to have anything to do with the task to which Macintosh summons them. It is a part of our main thesis that theology cannot longer postpone this encounter with metaphysics. We have been too long under the spell of Ritschlian escapism. But let theology come to this encounter with some self-respect and dignity, not asking from metaphysics a certainty which it cannot itself discover.

I suppose most of us must feel a disappointment. We have been deeply impressed with the success of the scientific method in the world of nature. Observation, experiment, and the inductive method have been the way to knowledge and power. Surely, we could study the working of God among people of faith, observe the results, and arrive at some certainties about God! All our hard-headed, factual, scientific natures were stirred by the possibilities. Now at last we would be freed from warring religious authorities, as well as from the misty uncertainties of speculative theology. Here we would catch God at work, plot the curves of His activity, and have all our questions answered. But for faith the results are, to say the least, disappointing. Our complaints about Macintosh's theology as an empirical science are three: (1) It is not scientific. (2) It is not empirical. (3) It is not theology.

1. It is not scientific. The classic methods of scientific experiment, as elaborated by J. S. Mill, are those of the joint method of agreement and difference and the method of concomitant variation. But how can these methods be applied to religious experience? The human factors that enter into religious experience are simply too complex to admit of any exact application of the method. How can any "controls" be established in religious experience? Consider the case of prayer. If a science of religion were really scientific, you should be able to show that the more faithful, regular, thoughtful, and sincere prayer is, that is, the more the religious adjustment is "right," the more clearly and inevitably would appear the benefits, the "answers" to prayer. Or to use the technical jargon of the logic of the social studies, we should have to discover a relatively high "coefficient of correlation." Some unit of measurement would have to be devised. That such improved adjustment is followed by clear results is often true. Yet the great mystics are the people who are baffled by the times of dryness in prayer. Who can say what human elements are missing? Not the mystics themselves! Further, the very fact that in all religious experience it is impossible to disentangle the human from the divine, makes any science of the divine element impossible.

To be sure, Macintosh does claim the method of Mill in his science. He disclaims that his can ever be an exact mathematical science. But he points to the fact that religious people do compare experiences. When they find reassurance

in the fact of an essential *agreement* with vast numbers of others as to the kind of *difference* (a divinely worthwhile difference) made in their experience by a divinely functioning Reality or Factor in response to a certain religious adjustment, they are using, in a crude way and without realizing it, the best of all the methods of inductive inference, namely, the well-known "joint method of agreement and difference." [35]

But the resemblance is at best crude and must remain so for any scientific theology, if only for the lack of any unit of measurement, however inexact. What objective, scientific basis can be afforded for comparing the satisfactions of human need through prayer? That there is a basis of comparison is essential to any talk between Christians about their experience. But the comparison is remote from any scientific method.

Moreover, science has no use for values subjectively considered. The biologist does take into account what is useful in the environment for the organism. This is objective, observable value. Scientific methods can be used in the study of ethics, logic, and aesthetics. But such methods have their strict limitations. The valuing subject, which is the *locus* of all values, eludes scientific study.

Of course, even the most abstract science is based on internal meaning, subjective interest. But its external meaning is always in the outward, the observable. Its field of study is not subjective value, but objective process. Its subjective interest is to avoid all but the most refined subjective interest. It has a very wholesome, inherited dread of value. In all his empirical laws Macintosh uses the expression "right religious adjustment." But "right" is no term of science except in the logical or mathematical sense. As G. F. Thomas has pointed out,[36] "right" for Macintosh is obviously Christian. But for the Buddhist, or for the Hindu, a quite different adjustment would condition a quite different response. Descriptive science would then be compelled (1) to discover the inner meaning of these various adjustments (this type of meaning being inaccessible to scientific study); (2) to discover the fidelity or dependability of the results, again relying on subjective reports which are not open to scientific verification; and (3) to discover, if possible, the comparative dependability of the various faiths to impart, for example, peace of mind, or ethical strength, and (4) in the light of this study to offer a comparative criticism of (a) the adjustment and (b) the response. When you undertake to study the comparative ethical results of the various religions, you are again relying on "norms" that are not scientific. This comparative study has been going on for some time. It should and will be continued. And while one of the requirements is impartiality in treating the claims of other faiths, it is safe to say that no student of comparative religions can ever approximate the objectivity of the man of science.

Science does not reason from phenomena to trans-empirical agents or beings. Indeed, philosophers whose training is in science tend to deny the existence of any causes that transcend what Kant called the world of "possible experience." Macintosh, however, reasons from religious effects in experience to a being or beings beyond all experience and calls to his aid his realistic theory of knowledge. Here he is already beyond the limits of science.

Again, there is a vast difference between religious faith and any scientific hypothesis. Some writers have been deceived by a superficial resemblance between them. An hypothesis is considered seriously as a possible explanation. But it is held tentatively, awaiting confirmation of its logical consequences, amendment, or rejection by the test of observation and experiment. The man's method is at stake, but not the man himself. Faith that is mere hypothesis is not faith but belief. Faith stakes not merely my opinions but my self, my whole being. This kind of faith is recognized by Macintosh as an essential element of his "right religious adjustment." Without it, the laws of his "scientific theology" could never be formulated. Faith has at heart the kind of certainty no scientist would ever think of admitting to any hypothesis, until it has been confirmed by experiment.

2. Mr. Macintosh's method is not empirical. Most empiricism is a pretense. It purports to rely only on the testimony of experience, while hidden assumptions of many kinds are used surreptitiously to add both content and form to the "experience." Hume was the most honest, the most relentless of all empiricists and he ended in complete skepticism. Macintosh's claim to be empirical is vitiated by (1) his dependence upon a realistic theory of knowledge which, in spite of all that he says, is still a postulate, (2) his preoccupation with human values, (3) his resolution to remain as far as possible within the Christian tradition, and (4) his reasoning from dependable results to a divine Factor as the cause of those results. On strictly empirical grounds, all that he is justified in saying is that when a man takes a right religious attitude, he takes a right religious attitude. In making the meager assertion that such a right religious attitude "tends" to be followed by the desired response, even with no reference as to the cause, he has already left the realm of the strictly empirical, since some trans-empirical observer is necessary to observe the "tendency." To *pure* empiricism all that is possible is the old tautology, $A = A$.[37]

3. Mr. Macintosh's system is not theology. It is rather anthropology—the study of human values and human experience. Theology is concerned with God, His Word, His purpose, His nature. While scientific accuracy is not possible for the student of theology as it is for the physicist, simply because a larger and more vital area of internal meaning is involved in the study of God, yet the theologian must preserve a hardy and an honest respect for objective fact. This is a hard saying, yet I believe it to be true: the hard-headed skeptic who is a brave son of fact is nearer the Kingdom of God than the theologian who, instead of serving God for His **own** sake, anxiously calls on God to preserve his own values.

If theology ever abandons this preoccupation with God it will lose its right to exist. It will then become subservient to human values and to the humanistic study of these values.

A theology which borrows its first principles from sociology, psychology or ethics has become a part of one of these sciences, and, since it has no independent point of view or object, the results of its researches have been determined from the start. It is vain to expect any new knowledge from such a science.[38]

While Macintosh seeks to discover God through human experience, his search is doomed to failure from the start, precisely because his primary field of inquiry is that of the human values of the true, the good, the beautiful. God then becomes a "dependable factor" in our experience. This means that we have an independent knowledge of these values, apart from God, and that these values are in a sense determinative of God. There is a vast difference between saying, "He is good and therefore God," and "He is God and therefore good."

As such a servant of the good and as a "dependable factor" in our experience, God becomes an instrument of our human ends. It is true that Macintosh makes a valiant attempt to keep man in the position of servant. He speaks of "self-surrender to God," and of God who causes human personality to "emerge" and who "educates" and "takes the initiative" in bringing man to appreciate true values. But his preoccupation with human values, his persistent use of the word "Factor," shows where the center of interest lies. It is in man. Biblical religion, on the other hand, asks that God be loved and served for His own sake and not used as a mere means to human ends, however noble or spiritual those ends may be. It makes the claim that it is in this service of God for His own sake that man fulfills his highest destiny.

In plain truth none of our human values can be taken as a fixed point in our thinking about God. Our idea of the true, our conception of the moral good, our feelings of the beautiful—what discerning mind can ever claim any finality for them? Our truth—it is perverted by our partial perspective which we brashly erect into a universal. Our goodness—it is at best pretentious and showy. Our vision of the moral good cannot escape some perversion by our practice. Our beautiful—it finds expression by faithfully reflecting in art, music, and drama the chaotic despair of our culture. It is just these values of ours that desperately need redemption and "trans-valuation." How shall we recognize the truth when we encounter it? How shall we be brave enough to confront the really good, when it rebukes our pride and shatters our self-esteem? How shall our eyes become pure so that we can look on the truly beautiful? These are the first questions which a theology of values ought to face. To start with our values and to build a system upon them is simply to reverse the right method and to be condemned to confusion from the start.

The poverty of the empirical method is nowhere more fully illustrated than in Macintosh's doctrine of revelation-salvation. Consider what he says about revelation. As the object of nature reveals itself through the experience of the scientist, so God reveals Himself through the experience of those who make "right religious adjustment." There can be no other revelation. The revelation in the Scripture, and in Jesus Christ, is valid only insofar as it is reproducible in the experience of men today. Any knowledge that claims to be revealed and that is not subject to contemporary verification is no revelation.

In the same spirit, Macintosh is driven to consider Jesus as merely the supreme illustration of religious experience. He represents man at his best, because through his perfect religious adjustment God was able to do more for him than for any other human.

The divinity of Jesus was much more an achievement of his religious experience than a native endowment. . . . Moreover, this view of the divineness of Jesus is especially encouraging, since it shows us that some degree of essentially the same sort of achievement is within the range of present possibility for every sincere and aspiring individual who will begin to cultivate the same sort of personal religion.[39]

Objective theology should begin by asking where and how God has in fact revealed Himself. If God is really to reveal His purpose, not as a stone reveals its content to the geologist, but as a friend reveals his hidden meaning to me, then that revelation will not be a "dependable Factor" in my experience. He *may* choose His own time, and place, and method. And if He should choose, for reasons of His own which may be beyond my surmising, to reveal Himself supremely through His Son, then I would do well to listen to the voice of God in Jesus Christ, rather than making of him a helpful but not indispensable illustration of religious experience.

Or consider Macintosh's doctrine of salvation. It is based upon our human concept of justice. Through the "assisting grace" of God, or by the example of Jesus, or by persuasion of the fact of God's holy love, by one means or the other, the sinner is brought to repentance. His will is turned from sin to righteousness. He is now a new man, no longer capable of the sins which he has committed in the past. He is not now the same man who committed those former sins. To withhold forgiveness now would be an injustice.

Jesus could declare God's forgiveness of sin, and so can anyone who is able to discern the marks of true repentance, and who understands that in genuine repentance the will is so turned from the sin that it is not right to impute to the person at present the moral evil which he once indulged in, but which is not now characteristic of his will. By repenting he has not *earned* forgiveness; repentance alone does not make the wrong entirely right; it does not make objective amends for injury done. Forgiveness is still an *act of grace* on the part of the one who forgives, thereby refusing to let the past sin be a barrier to present fellowship. And yet the sincerely repentant ought to be granted forgiveness; to withhold it would be wrong.[40]

Which is it? Forgiveness by grace, or forgiveness because it ought to be granted? Both it cannot be.

This is not "justification by works," if by works we mean the perfunctory performance of external acts. (This is not what St. Paul meant by works.) Neither is it "justification by faith," if by "faith" we mean intellectual assent to doctrinal teaching. (Nor is this what St. Paul meant by faith.) It is justification by right decision, justification by the good will.[41]

This is as far as any doctrine of atonement can go if it is based on human experience. Yet if it is true we ought no longer to praise God for His amazing mercy. We ought rather to congratulate Him for His discernment!

How meager is this teaching for the man who sincerely repents! If repentance and faith are genuine, he will consent to no talk of his not being the same man who committed the former sins. He *is* a new man in Christ. But part of the old man lay in just this fault of irresponsible evasion, by which he carelessly disowned connection with his past sins. As a child of faith he becomes responsible for the first time. He knows that he is "and to the end of endless time shall remain, the doer of that wilfully traitorous deed." [42] There is, as Royce said with fine discernment, a "hell of the irrevocable" and its fires are not to be quenched by any talk of his being a different man now. This is the point from which the divine forgiveness begins.

Moreover, he has no jaunty confidence that now his will is turned irrevocably toward righteousness. As a child of faith, he will have confidence that God, who has forgiven him at unspeakable cost, and who has now accepted him as forgiven, will so much the more not leave the work of restoration half-finished.[43] Yet he knows, or will soon discover, that sin is not done with him. He may not fall into the old vices. But pride has its more subtle temptations, which are even more dangerous to the saint than to the sinner. All the more likely is he to fall into them, if he retains his pride that he has been justified by his own "right decision," by his own "good will."

That which is really powerful in moving the sinner to repentance is the very heart of Christ's atonement: that here God out of His great mercy exhibits Himself as bearing the full penalty, pay-ing the full price (the figures of speech cannot do justice to the reality) for man's sin. As a result it is possible for Him to be "righteous and that he justifies him who has faith in Jesus." [44] (This "and" is one of the most momentous words in the Bible.) It is this kind of grace that really moves us, that gives us peace of conscience and leaves us dwelling in the world of moral reality, without evasion. It leaves no room for human pride, no standing ground for boasting. When a man honestly turns from his pride and his pretense, this is the only kind of mercy that will really satisfy him. Yet this is the grace which we have no right to demand, which we can scarcely conceive. If we established it by our own proof, we should simply be guilty of the grossest moral presumption. If this forgiveness is to come to us, it can come to us through no discovery of our own, but only through a clear, unmistakable word from God. This is our basic need for revelation.

Macintosh made a valiant attempt to establish the "science of religion," for which William James called almost fifty years ago. While later students may use the empirical method and avoid some of Macintosh's mistakes, the major difficulties that we have singled out are inherent in the method itself. For bringing these imperfections to light, theology owes a debt of gratitude to Macintosh.

If we could discard his attempt at being "scientific," lay aside the pretense of empiricism, and restore some opportunity for God to speak other than through "dependable responses," there remains much that is of permanent worth in Macintosh's work. After all, it is to the level of our experience that the revelation of God must speak. It is safe to say that the Christian faith would be quickly forgotten if it were never verified in experience. Theological doctrine is a sterile business, unless it is translated into experience. The most persuasive argument for the Christian faith is still a changed life, the witness of the man in deeds, whose dogged assurance stands under all the questions of the learned, "One thing I know, that though I was blind, now I see." [45]

The Bible contains its own appeal to experience. "Oh taste and see that Jehovah is good." [46] "Prove me now herewith, saith Jehovah of hosts." [47]

Bless Jehovah, O my soul, and forget not all his benefits: who forgiveth all thine iniquities; who healeth all thy diseases; who redeemeth thy life from destruction; who crowneth thee with loving-kindness and tender mercies; who satisfieth thy desire with good things, so that thy youth is renewed like the eagle.[48]

When John the Baptist out of his prison and out of his doubt sent two messengers to Jesus with the question, "Are you he who is to come, or shall we look for another?" Jesus did not rebuke John for his lack of faith. He simply told the messengers, "Go and tell John what you have seen and heard." [49]

The Bible does not regard human experience with contempt. Yet that experience is one of frustration, self-contradiction, fear, defeat, despair, until turning from itself, it finds in the Word of God alone its salvation and its confidence.

CHAPTER 5

A Protestant and a Catholic Answer

Reason and experience, these are the two time-honored approaches to knowledge. Experience supplies us with the data of knowledge through sensation, the raw materials without which we could have no knowledge. Reason organizes, classifies, relates the materials of sensation, enabling us to live in a world instead of a chaos, giving us laws and hence the ability to predict. This is one of the clear results of modern philosophy. But when we use these familiar tools in the knowledge of God, we run into serious difficulty. Reason encounters limits beyond which it seems powerless to go. It is so much an instrument of the human situation, so bound by the limits of our own relative position, its categories so clearly adapted to our earth-born experience, that it is unable to establish the certainties that are essential to the life of faith.

On the other hand, the attempt to rely on experience and to draw out a science of divine truth has ended in disappointment and for much the same reason. What we find in religious experience is in part conditioned by what we want to find, in part by what we are capable of finding. We find some support for *our* ideals, which is very good as far as it goes. But it is just because our ideals are confused and distorted by our idolatry of self, just because these ideals, yes ourselves, need a clear judgment and a complete re-making, that we cannot answer faith's questions by an appeal to experience as such. The living God cannot be reduced to the status of an object in our field of experience. What we get is a "divine factor" in experience, whose "revelations" are like those of a plant to a botanist. We are thus in the frightfully insecure position of masters of the divine truth when we ought to be its servants. We are left weltering in our own subjectivity, since the truth we receive is conditioned by our own capacity to receive and understand. Elsewhere must we look for the knowledge of God.

Do the exponents of faith have the answer? In recent times the most valiant and persuasive attempt to free faith from the restraints of reason has been made by Karl Barth. His general position should be well known, though it is often misunderstood, if not misrepresented. God is the real Sovereign of our days, God in the highest, God who is a mystery to man. Man is a creature and this creaturely status is reflected even in man's best thinking. That is why Barth is opposed to natural theology. All that the arguments can give us are just gods, made in the image of man, reflecting at best man's imperfections. That is why Barth sees the "humor and fragility" of rational attempts to search out God. God alone can speak. His Word has been spoken in truth and grace through Jesus Christ. Theology is man's reasoned attempt to understand what is said in that Word.

Man's sin is his self-assertion against God, his turning away from the divine grace, his exaltation of the self into the place of God. Consequently man's truth is distorted because he idolatrously erects his finite perspective into a universal, insists that God and man ought to see life through his eyes, recognize his limited perspective as the favored one. This basic sin leaves man in deep anxiety over his own security, since he knows that he cannot manage the world so as to make his own position safe. This anxiety in turn perverts and distorts both his relations to his fellowmen and his understanding of the truth. This sin has become so much a part of man that he cannot even understand what his sin is, much less be freed from it, until God has spoken His Word of grace and healing.

From this it follows that man the thinker is also man the sinner. As it is not possible for man to *do* anything that is pleasing to God, so it is impossible for man to *think* anything that is pleasing to Him. Our creaturehood and our sin mean that when we reason about

God, our thought is vitiated by pride and by the subtle pretension that by its reasoning would control God and use Him for our human purposes. To attach religious value to even our loftiest thinking about God is a kind of idolatry. Faith is therefore the freedom to hear the Word of God, and in that Word to receive not only our salvation but our truth as well.

Barth does not use gentle language in talking about natural theology.

When a man is occupied with genuine theology, he will always regard the so-called natural theology as an abyss. If he does not want to fall into it he will not go near it. In horror and indignation he will turn his back on it as the great temptation and fountain of errors. He does not meddle with it. . . . In the complete repudiation of natural theology, one does not first stare at a snake, in order to continue to stare, until he is hypnotized and is then really bitten by it. When he first sees it he strikes it with his walking stick and strikes it dead! [1]

It must be clear that the faith by which we receive the Word is not our own doing. We dare not be proud of our faith. Human pride is so persistent, so subtle, that it must be left no least ground on which to stand. Our faith itself is the gift of the Holy Spirit. Our faith is *in* God, not ourselves. In his controversy with Barth in the mid-thirties, Brunner had complained that Barth had not done justice to man the thinking believer. Brunner distinguished between the formal and material *imago Dei* in man. In the formal sense man is both a subject of experience and responsible, even though a sinner. While in the material sense the image of God has been deformed by sin and nothing in him has escaped the defilement of sin, in the formal sense the image of God is intact. God can speak to man, even though he is a sinner.

That there is a point of contact for the divine saving grace, no one can deny who recognizes that not stones or blocks, but only the human subject can receive the Word of God and the Holy Spirit. The point of contact is this—that in the sinner the formal image of God is not destroyed, his manhood, his humanity, and the two features mentioned above: his capacity for the Word of God and his responsibility.[2]

So when faith is born the subject in his self-consciousness is not destroyed. The act of saving faith is carefully distinguished from the ecstasy of the mystic. "While the Bible calls faith the work and the gift of the Holy Spirit, yet it never says, the Holy Spirit believes in me. But I believe through the Holy Spirit." [3]

Barth agrees that man is and remains a subject of experience. But when that fact is extended to include man's capacity for revelation in responsibility he senses danger.

This presupposition, this fact of being a person, is not destroyed through sin. . . . In fact not, we shall say. Man as sinner is also man and no turtle. But is his reason therefore "competent" to determine the nature of God, as of anything else in the world? What has man's being man to do with "capacity for revelation"? Would not a man who had just been saved from drowning by a competent swimmer appear ridiculous if he ascribed his "capacity for being rescued" to the incontrovertible fact that he is a man and not a block of lead? Perhaps he could then reassure himself that he had assisted his rescuer with a few swimming motions of his own! Can that be Brunner's meaning? No, for we heard of "Man, who of himself can do nothing for his salvation." Also, according to Brunner, "the possibility of doing anything pleasing in the sight of God" is destroyed. Should that not apply above all to the capacity for receiving God's revelation? . . . What does he then mean by "capacity for revelation"? Why should it be that the obvious fact that man as sinner is also a responsible person—though strictly within the limits of the formal sense of the word!—serves in the least to understand the revelation as something else than Divine grace? Can Brunner say a single word beyond that obvious fact without contradicting his unqualified affirmation of the Reformation principle of *sola scriptura—sola gratia?* [4]

More recently Barth puts the matter more simply. Of course there is a subjective side of belief. "I believe," says the Creed. But it was not a good thing when man became preoccupied with the uplift and emotion of his own believing experience rather than with the God in whom he believes. This is the thwarting of faith itself.

By my believing I see myself completely filled and determined by this object of my faith. And what interests me is not myself with my faith, but He in whom I believe. And then I learn that by thinking of Him and looking to Him, my interests are also best provided for.[5]

When we turn from much recent liberal theology, and its pre-occupation with the swamplands of the subjective, we find vigor and clarity in Barth. It is refreshing to be directed from man to God. It is not surprising that Barth has had a profound influence upon both European and American theology in the last thirty years. It is safe now to say that at least a minor reformation in theology is to be dated from the publication of his *Commentary on Romans* in 1919. And it is clear that the scientific temper, with its search for the objective, should recognize a kindred spirit in Barth who turns away from subjective opinions to the outward fact, the Object of faith and knowledge.

There has been significant development in Barth's thought. In his recent works he is clear that reason has a central place in the life of faith, a recognition that was obscured at the time of his controversy with Brunner. To be sure, it is a regenerate reason, devoted to a Truth that transforms all our truths. It is not an extension of man's natural knowledge. The Apostle Paul seemed to give warrant to natural theology.

For what can be known about God is plain to them, because God has shown it to them. Ever since the creation of the world his invisible nature, namely, his eternal power and deity, has been clearly perceived in the things that have been made. So they are without excuse.[6]

Here is Barth's early comment on this passage:

We know that God is He whom we do not know, and that our ignorance is precisely the problem and the source of our knowledge. We know that God is the Personality which we are not, and that this lack of Personality is precisely what dissolves and establishes our personality. The recognition of the absolute heteronomy under which we stand is itself an autonomous recognition; and this is precisely *that which may be known of God.*[7]

Barth has never modified this position, except that today he would probably say that even this "autonomous recognition" could only take place in a regenerate mind.

But he does not despise the power of reason.

The saying, "Despise only reason and science, man's supremest power of all," was uttered not by a prophet, but by Goethe's Mephisto. Christendom and the theological world were always ill-advised in thinking it their duty for some reason or other, either of enthusiasm or of theological conception, to betake themselves to the camp of an opposition to reason. . . . Faith is knowledge; it is related to God's Logos, and is therefore a thoroughly logical matter.[8]

Christian knowledge, he continues, is more akin to *sophia* and *sapientia* than to *scientia*. But genuine rational interests are never denied for the sake of faith. Rather by faith God confers upon us the Truth in Christ, to which all our understanding is now to conform.

Moreover, in all theology Barth recognizes man's relative position. Its success will always depend upon "the state of the Church at different times." It is a critical study, and the authority of church dogma will therefore never be absolute. "Christian dogmatics will always be a thinking, an investigation and an exposition which are relative and liable to error." Barth looks forward to later men in the hope that they "may think and say better and more profoundly what we were endeavouring to think and to say." [9]

Barth is also now more concerned with the problem of communication. How shall the man of faith speak to the man who knows not our Christian faith? Brunner had argued that in its proclamations the Church must seek out from human words those that are most appropriate to the Word of God. "What I shall say to a man on his death bed is a holy matter; but how I shall say it, so that it reaches him, is not less a holy matter." [10]

To this Barth replied:

As for preaching, I have the strongest impression that I best reach and "interest" my hearers when I reckon to the minimum with what already "answers" to the Word of God; when I forsake the notion that one "can" preach this Word; when I rely as little as possible on the art of "reaching" people through the means of my speech, when I rather let my preaching be shaped and stamped and rendered adequate to what the text wants to say to me.[11]

But now Barth recognizes the importance of the *how* as well as the *what* of preaching. The Church, he says, must be bilingual. It speaks its own language, the "language of Canaan," since that alone is appropriate to its message.

Therefore the language of faith, the language of public responsibility in which as Christians we are bound to speak, will inevitably be the language of the Bible, the Hebrew and the Greek Bible and the translations of them, and the language of Christian tradition, the language in the forms of the thoughts, concepts and ideas, in which in the course of centuries the Christian Church has gained and upheld and declared its knowledge.[12]

To surrender this language of faith is to renounce the freedom of Christian witness and to join "the fellowship of the quiet."

Yet this is not enough. The Church stands in the midst of a world that understands not the language of faith. In such a world the Church cannot keep silent. The world might be relieved of some embarrassment if the Church would sing its praises within its own walls and in its esoteric language. The Church must translate its message into the language of the world, yes, into the language of the newspaper.

Where confession is serious and clear, it must be fundamentally translatable into the speech of Mr. Everyman, the man and woman in the street, into the language of those who are not accustomed to reading Scripture and singing hymns, but who possess a quite different vocabulary and quite different spheres of interest.[13]

Moreover, the Church's message must reach the whole man, man in all his socio-economic, racial, and political relations, for this is the real man. Barth chides the German Church for keeping silent in 1933, although there was much genuine Christian confession at that time—in the language of the Church. But the Church should also have spoken in the language of politics. If so, "it would have become clear that the Evangelical Church had to say 'No' to National Socialism, 'No' from its very roots." [14]

But "translation" means coming to grips with the thought forms of the world. Earlier Brunner had insisted that Christian thought had to encounter the thought of the world and in doing so it would have to rely on natural theology and appeal to human responsibility. But at the time Barth would not allow this. In talking to unbelievers you spoke your own language of faith and left the bewildered unbeliever to understand you as best he could.

According to my experience, you can best speak to "intellectuals," "unbelievers" and modern youth when, instead of catechizing out of them their capacity for revelation, as though their opposition to Christianity were not really of serious significance, you deal with them in all quietness and simplicity (remembering that Christ died and rose again also for them). Then you can make yourself understood to them, because they see you actually standing where you claim to stand as an evangelical theologian, on the ground of the doctrine of justification through faith alone.[15]

It is precisely at this point that the next step in Barth's development should occur. What does this "translation" into the language of the world mean? It means searching the mind of our day, understanding skepticism *from the inside*, in order to find a point of contact for the Christian message. But this involves an appeal to human thinking and leads straight to what Brunner in 1935 called "a Christian natural theology," whose best exemplar may yet turn out to be Augustine. Such an appeal need not imply the validity of any natural human inferences about the nature of God, any more than a teacher explaining the methods of science to a class of beginners concedes that the non-scientific mentality of his students is adequate. To speak the language of the world does not mean the denial of revelation, or that the human mind is capable by the extension of its own limited categories of encompassing the reality of God.

Is there danger that in this translation into the language of the world the hearer should misunderstand? It seems one of the necessary risks of faith. Yet it was a risk which the prophets did not hesitate to take, a risk that Jesus constantly took and even recognized in his parable of the sower, a risk that God Himself took in speaking His Word through His Son. In fact here is the fulness of divine grace that God in His mercy stoops to speak in a universal human language, in a Man. Here is the clearest and most eloquent of all language, yet a Word that still remains a hidden mystery to countless men, including men of remarkable moral and intellectual insight.

Consider the nature of a word. It is not properly a word when it is merely spoken or written. It fulfills itself only when it is heard and understood. A word is a flash of understanding between two minds. If it has no meaning to the hearer it is nonsense. This holds true even when God speaks to man. If the Gospel is to be preached, it must be clothed in human language, sometimes using words that are soiled in the marketplace. It must direct itself to human meaning as it happens to be and it thus implies some capacity to receive and understand. The internal meaning of the hearer may be one of confidence or despair. If the Word of God is to reach him it must connect somewhere with his meaning, appeal to his reason, even if it be to condemn, negate, remake and redeem the whole world of man's meaning. It is just the failure of the Church to understand the mind of its own time, to connect with the thought of its day, to find the appropriate "translation," that ought to burden the conscience of every Christian thinker. We need to ask these questions: what goes on in a man's mind when he turns from unbelief to faith? And what reasonable, yes, logical, road must a man travel in order that he may be open to the faith-evoking Word?

But one thing is clear and Barth seems to recognize it. If man's dependence upon divine grace has any meaning, if the grace of God is to be a governing factor in his daily decisions, and if he is in any way to try to communicate his faith, or even to talk about it, then he must mean something; his external meaning points to outward fact as surely as it does when he studies a law in chemistry. Faith and reason fulfill themselves only by working together in full recognition of their mutual dependence. Faith without reason is not only blind; it is empty. Only in this recognition does faith do justice to itself and recover its right to become articulate.

But another answer has been made to the dualism of faith and knowledge, an answer so impressive in its philosophic weight, that we cannot longer postpone its consideration. It is the answer of Thomas Aquinas and his modern interpreters. The Thomist synthesis of Aristotelian thought and Christian revelation is largely determinative for modern Roman Catholic thought. Aquinas did not doubt that reason is capable of demonstrating certain truths about God. Just as the will is not completely corrupted by sin, so reason still retains some powers of the original *imago Dei*. Reason was wounded by sin and suffers from each fresh wound that sin inflicts upon it. But as Etienne Gilson explains, "The very essence of human reason was left intact and even the natural aptitude of man to know the truth has suffered less from original sin than his aptitude to will the good." [16]

This contrasts with the view of the Reformers. While Calvin spent some effort to show that God had revealed Himself in His works, this "is insufficient to conduct us into the right way. Some sparks, indeed, are kindled, but smothered before they have emitted any great degree of light." [17] As against the position of Barth, Gilson points to the insights of Aristotle about which "both St. Thomas and Calvin can do nothing." What Aristotle discovered about God was by the natural reason and without the help of faith.

One first being, the supreme principle and cause of nature, source of all intelligibility, of all order, and of all beauty, who eternally leads a life of happiness, because, being thought itself, it is an eternal contemplation of its own thought, all that was taught by Aristotle; and if we compare his theology to the ancient mythologies we will see at a glance what immense progress human reason had made since the era of Chronos and Jupiter without the aid of Christian Revelation. [18]

Human reason can do as much today, concludes Gilson, without the aid of revelation.

The Thomists have great confidence in the arguments and are inclined to attribute any dissent to defective ability in philosophy. "The thinker who has seen and grasped the proof has no need of authority. . . . (The existence of God) is a proved fact." [19] What is known is no longer believed. Knowledge has replaced faith. And since the direct knowledge of God is one of the central elements in the beatific vision, so every growth from faith to knowledge is a gain. Referring to the text, "Seek and ye shall find," Augustine had said, "What is believed, not known, can not be said to be found: and no one is fitted to find God, unless he shall have believed beforehand that he will know." [20]

But St. Thomas and his modern interpreters recognize limits in the human knowledge of God. (1) We cannot know the essence of God, *what* He is; we can only know His existence, *that* He is. And insofar as we can know any of the attributes of God, we must rely on the methods of negation and of analogy. The Catholic philosopher has a clear awareness of the majesty of God, and knows that human arguments say little. But the little that is said is clear and highly important.

(2) Moreover, the philosophic quest is a long one. St. Thomas, with a high respect for philosophy, says that many years are required to be a philosopher. Knowledge is therefore limited to the few who have competence. For the philosopher in the long years before he reaches certainty, and for the many who have not the competence or the leisure for the quest, faith will guide the way.

(3) Faith supplies reason with its objectives. It is ready at hand "to assist the spontaneous inferences of reason in surviving the eventual shipwreck of their demonstration." [21] It is preposterous to expect that a Catholic philosopher will divest himself of his faith.

(4) The most important truths about God are beyond reason and must therefore be received by faith. Such are the Trinity, the Incarnation, the Atonement, the Resurrection, etc.

St. Thomas renounced the ontological argument of Anselm for two principal reasons. (1) The essence of God is unknown to the natural reason of man. If we could know the essence of God then His existence could be proved, since in God essence and existence are one. In fact there are many peoples who have not conceived God as the being than which a greater could not be conceived. No, human knowledge must start with sensible objects and follow the laws of thought. The arguments, therefore, claim an empirical basis. They profess to be *a posteriori*, that is they argue from effect to cause. (2) Existence does not follow conception, however necessary to conception. If the being, than whom a greater cannot be conceived, really exists, then His existence is necessary. But we cannot thus prove His existence.

The arguments are more fully stated in the opening chapters of the *Summa Contra Gentiles*. In their more compact form they appear in *Summa Theologica*, Part I, Question 2. They rest heavily on Aristotle.

1. The first "way" starts with the observed fact of motion, including as the term did for Aristotle, not merely change of place but qualitative change as well. Now motion requires explanation. What is in motion, or undergoing change, must be set in motion by another.

Movement is the passage from potency to act, therefore to be moved is to be in potency, and to move is precisely the contrary, it is to be in act. Now the same thing in the same respect cannot be both in potency and in act, and therefore everything which is moved is incapable of moving itself, and must therefore be moved by another.[22]

To deny the validity of this argument is, as these writers often remind us, to violate the logical law of non-contradiction. But what sets in motion is itself moved by another. But an infinite regress is impossible since without a first mover nothing would ever be in motion. "Therefore it is necessary to arrive at a first mover, put in motion by no other; and this everyone understands to be God." [23]

Against the infinite regress it is argued that it explains nothing. It simply pushes the difficulty back so far as to be out of sight and out of mind. For unless the prime mover is involved, no motion could have been started. Or in slightly different form, if the conditions of a given single event were infinite in number, then an infinite series would have to be completed in order that the effect could exist. But a completed infinite series is a contradiction in terms.

It should be noted that this argument implies Aristotle's doctrine that motion is impelled, like the throwing of a rock, and therefore not merely the beginning but the continuation of motion needs explanation. The Newtonian concept of inertia is an embarrassment to this argument. At any rate the modern naturalist is quite willing to work with the idea of an infinite regress and if this leaves the whole process unexplained he may ask, "By what right do you ask an explanation?" Motion itself may be the ultimate. To him at least the argument is not convincing.

2. The second argument is based on the fact of contingent existence which requires an efficient cause. A thing cannot be its own efficient cause since then it would have to exist prior to itself. We are therefore driven to trace the causes back to a first efficient cause, which is God. Again, St. Thomas argues, there cannot be an infinite regress since without a cause there can be no effect and without a first cause all subsequent effects would be impossible. But more than an infinite regress in time is involved, since causes are hierarchically arranged and you must therefore come to a supreme cause.

Against the charge of Kant, that in the causal argument men escape from experience into transcendental concepts, one writer argues that this is simply not true.[24] We go right back to experience again. From the experience of the contingency of all caused beings we can argue to the necessity of the uncaused cause. And since God is necessary He cannot have the imperfections of contingent beings. By the way of negation we can thus prove that God is eternal, simple (without composition of parts), immaterial, unlimited pure actuality. By the way of analogy we can also prove that in Him exist all the perfections found in the effects. But, the writer persists, this is argument from experience. Another writer maintains that the only alternative to this proof is "identifying non-reality with reality, non-being with being," [25] (assuming that a caused being is "non-reality.") The reader who has followed our analysis of Kant's criticism of Anselm's argument will have no difficulty in recognizing the ontologism implicit in these interpretations of Aquinas.

3. The third argument is based on the contingency of all created things. Since that which has possible being at some time does not exist, if all reality had only this possible being, at some time nothing at all would exist. But from universal nothingness no being could come into existence. Therefore something must exist not merely as a possible but as a necessary being, whose necessity is from itself. This being is God. It will be seen that this is close to Anselm's argument as is the one that follows.

4. The fourth argument is based on degrees in truth and being. It is an observed fact that there are degrees of goodness, truth, nobility, etc. But as the word "hotter" has meaning only by reference to the hottest, so the better implies the best, the nobler the noblest, the more true the most true. But according to Aristotle, that which possesses the greatest truth also has the greatest being. The supremely true is also supreme being, the cause of all excellences in other things. And this being is called God.[26]

One interpreter explains that any being, in which truth, goodness, nobility, etc., are found in a diminished degree, cannot be the cause of these perfections. We must look to that being in which they exist undiminished.[27] Another argues that this fourth "way" is not ontological, since it starts from the "*fact* of multiplication and gradation of imperfections," [28] not from the idea of imperfection.

5. The fifth argument is that from design. As the arrow is directed by the archer, so natural bodies incapable of thought are plainly directed toward their end.

Out of these five arguments come not merely the knowledge of God's existence but of certain of His attributes as well. He is eternal, infinite, immutable, pure actuality, spirit, without parts, self-existent, and contains absolute goodness, truth, and whatever other perfections may be found in man.

It will be seen that all the arguments are variations of the causal argument. The validity of all the arguments rests therefore on the causal category. The Thomists insist that causality is learned from experience. Yet at just this point Hume's analysis gives us pause. What do we learn from experience about cause and effect? And if we are to use the causal category as an ultimate principle we run into Kant's criticism. In spite of the Thomists' appeal to experience it is clear that we are making causation a "transcendental concept." Even if we can ignore Hume's searching criticism and escape Kant's critical philosophy, we cannot pretend that we really understand what causation is. The arguments are thereby weakened as proof.

It is also clear that the Thomists cannot escape ontologism. If Anselm's argument were merely from idea to existence the escape would be easy. But as we have seen, the real question at issue is whether necessity of thought implies necessity of being. Take the necessities of thought out of the Thomist arguments and they collapse.

It is further clear that the God of the arguments, pure thought, unmoved mover, pure actuality, is not the God of the Bible. But to say, as some Protestant writers do, that the God of the arguments bears no resemblance to the God of the Bible is extreme and it is insincere to pretend that the assurance of the arguments would have no value for faith. But with all that the arguments might conceivably establish, the most important questions would still be unanswered.

The most serious difficulty with the Thomistic treatment is the intellectualist conception of faith that is implicit in all this discussion. Faith is equated with belief. Faith is the acceptance of a body of divine truth on the authority of the Church as the interpreter of the Scriptures. For the New Testament, however, faith is directed through and beyond the Scriptures to God and is a personal relationship. When faith is centered on anything less, it is depersonalized and robbed of its central meaning. This is an attempt to read external meaning apart from internal meaning and constitutes one of the most serious errors in Catholic theology. It need scarcely be added that the Protestant share in this error is widespread.

As we shall see, it is only when faith and reason are both restored to their rightful place as functions of personal encounter that they are freed from distortion. The work of God through the Holy Spirit is personal. The personal God meets man as a person and in a personal way. Any sincere believer will confess to great mystery in the work of the Holy Spirit. But to lower that work to a subpersonal level is to reduce faith to a form of magic. And only when reason is seen in its personal implications is it freed from its wanderings into abstractions and contradictions, and brought to its fulfillment.

CHAPTER 6

Our Knowledge of Persons

One difficulty has been lurking in our argument from the beginning. We have been feeling rather than detecting its presence. It is time that we brought this hidden thing to light, for it is concealed not only in our argument; it pervades the whole of modern thought. In our ordinary experience we use the word knowledge in the broadest sense. Yet when we come to define it, we invariably define exact, scientific knowledge. Descartes and Spinoza frankly accepted this mathematical ideal. Its certainty was so clear and compelling that they proposed to find the same clarity in all knowledge. The ideal persists. All the physical sciences have been seeking to state their results in mathematical form. The social sciences have envied and imitated the exact sciences. The results have been so impressive that today every school boy learns that mathematical truth is truth *par excellence*. Our whole culture is dominated by this ideal. To prove anything means to reduce it to mathematical law. Certainty is mathematical exactness. Any conclusion that does not conform to this standard is condemned to the outer darkness of the doubtful and the suspect.

Now this kind of knowledge is highly desirable in making machine tools, in predicting a chemical reaction, in preventing disease, or in testing the accuracy of a syllogism. But it has its limitations, too. It may turn out to be an inept device in the knowledge of other human beings, or of God. It sets rigid forms and excludes as knowledge all that does not fit its standards. It prejudges the case. A school of contemporary philosophy simply rejects as meaningless all claims to knowledge that are not capable of scientific verification. Even Kant drew up his table of categories with the sciences of mathematics and physics in mind. These categories set the limits of "possible experience" beyond which knowledge could not go without contradiction.

The method has had disastrous consequences for religious thought. Men brought this hunger for mathematical exactness to their religious quest and sought to make the Living God conform to their method and answer their questions. The results? Either a God who was just a concept of our own constructing, or a God about whom nothing could be known. In either case there was no way to find certainty. In the meantime men bent their efforts and devoted their lives to those aspects of reality in which they could walk with confident steps. They could feel sure about science. It enabled them to predict and therefore gave them power over nature.

It should be clear that mathematics gains its certainty at a price—abstraction. Indeed, the highest certainties have no direct relation to experience at all. They are arithmetical or geometric constructions in the mind. The results are highly useful for science. But they are achieved with scarcely any empirical reference. At the other end of the scale is the fully concrete. It is found in our fullest experiences. It is where in company with my fellows I deal with the world of nature. Or more exactly, it is where I meet my fellowman against the background of nature and in the presence of God. The most concrete experiences are those to which I must respond with the whole man. In such experiences I have knowledge, but a knowledge that overflows the limits of scientific exactness.[1]

We can clarify this difficulty by arranging a table of the various branches of human knowledge, with the most exact science at one end of the scale and the least exact at the other. The scale will be something like this:

FORMAL SCIENCES	mathematics logic
PHYSICAL SCIENCES	{ physics chemistry astronomy geology
	the biological sciences
SOCIAL STUDIES	{ history economics political science psychology sociology anthropology
	ethics aesthetics philosophy theology

As we study this table some arresting facts begin to be clear.

(1) Each science selects certain aspects of experience for its study and neglects all others as irrelevant to its purposes. This is what we mean by abstraction. It is an indispensable part of the scientific method. Our first discovery from our table is this: exactness is in direct proportion to the degree of abstraction. Mathematics, the most abstract of the forms of knowledge, is likewise the most exact. Physics and chemistry fall just short of mathematics in exactness and abstractness. The biological sciences are more concrete and less exact. The social sciences are more concrete and still less able to reduce their findings to mathematics, just because they must take into account the ambiguities and mysteries of the human personality. Recent physics has modified its claim to mathematical exactness under the influence of the quantum theory and Heisenberg's principle of indeterminacy. Individual electrons are not entirely predictable. But by taking a multitude (fair sample) of electrons into account their individual variations cancel each other out and prediction now becomes a matter of

reading statistical averages.[2] This looks like the statistical method used in the social sciences. But careful analysis will reveal that statistical averages both describe and predict behavior much more accurately in the physical than in the social sciences.

(2) The more exact sciences are generally the older. This sometimes leads to the illusion that when the newer sciences are as old as physics they will be as exact. Biology sometimes tries to reduce itself to biochemistry, but does so at the cost of neglecting some aspects of the living organism. Psychology often tries to be experimental and biological. This has been a highly fruitful development. As long as the psychologist knows what he is doing, and does not claim that such outer aspects of the human person as his reaction times are the whole of him, there is no dispute between religion and psychology. Greater exactness is highly desirable in every science, as long as it is kept in mind that exactness always pays the price of narrowing the field of interest. Aristotle's warning still holds that it is not wise to look in any field for more exactness than the subject matter warrants.[3]

(3) All science seeks to free itself from subjective bias and aims at "objectivity." The success of science has been achieved in part by eliminating from its vocabulary words that are heavy with anthropomorphic and emotional overtones and the substitution of impersonal symbols. "Force" suggests the activity of the human will and is therefore less desirable than "energy." The best symbol of all is the mathematical equation. Objectivity is never the complete suppression of subjective interest, for that would be suicidal. Nor is it mere corroboration by sense experience, as the empiricists sometimes hold. The physical sciences are making less use of the senses, more of mathematical construction in verification. But objectivity does mean social corroboration. "The life-blood of science is distrust of individual belief as such." [4] No scientist regards the results of an experiment as assured until the experiment has been repeated and the results confirmed by another observer. Now this standard of objectivity is most completely fulfilled in the exact sciences, is less and less attainable as sciences become more

concrete. Objectivity in a chemical analysis, where another can check my findings, is one thing. It is quite another thing to achieve objectivity in a complex economic and social issue where the security of my class and of my own family is involved. As knowledge becomes more concrete, internal meaning and subjective interest become more intense. We have only to note the bitterness of controversy among psychologists, economists, and sociologists, not to mention theologians and philosophers, and to recall that such controversies have no comparable violence among physicists and chemists. Objectivity in these vital matters is much more difficult to achieve, involves not merely comparing observations, but reconciliation of interests as well. As we move toward the concrete sciences, objectivity is purchased at an increasingly high moral price.

But this deference to the other observer in the physical sciences, even while progressively depersonalizing their symbols, this increasingly important appeal to the internal meaning of others in the concrete sciences, brings us face to face with our difficulty. How do we know other minds in mathematical terms? The answer is, we don't. This is the embarrassing question, the hidden skeleton in the closet, of modern philosophy.

How do I know my neighbor's mind? How do I know that my neighbor's mind exists? The questions seem foolish: of course, we know other minds. But how do we know them? We know things of nature through *outer* senses, said John Locke, and our own thoughts and feelings through an *inner sense*. But he mentioned no sense by which I can know my neighbor's mind. Nor for that matter has any other philosopher. Yet they have wrestled with the problem again and again. Knowledge of other minds we surely have. Yet no one has been able to explain it. They have argued that we infer the reality of our neighbor's mind by analogy. I know that my thought moves my body, my ideas are uttered by my tongue, my hands are expressive of certain feelings. When I see his body behaving in a similar way I infer that this action comes from a mind. The argument ought to be abandoned, for it does not describe what actually takes place. It is not thus that I know that my neighbor's mind exists.

Is it then by response to our questions, by customary signs such as speech and laughter, that we recognize the existence of other minds? The signs teach us much about our neighbors. But they are after all only physical signs. Royce said that we know the reality of our fellows because of the ideas we get from them. They "furnish us with the constantly needed supplement to our own fragmentary meanings." [5]

It is one of the basic certainties that we do know other minds. Let us consider how we *know* that we know them.

(1) We would have no knowledge of material objects without other minds. It is simply not true to say that we begin with a knowledge of nature, develop a sense of our own body, then reason from my neighbor's bodily behavior to the existence of his mind. That is to reverse the actual order. It is through my neighbor's mind that I learn that there is an objective world—out there! It is not merely that we derive our language, the instrument of our thought, from others. It is not merely that scientists rely on independent confirmation to establish their needed objectivity. It is much more basic than that. I believe in the reality of a physical object before me not merely from my own senses, but from the fact that I see other people treating this object as real. It was from another, probably my mother, that I learned to trust my senses, and what is more important, to interpret them. Without human companionship it is doubtful that we would have any more of a world of objects than has a rat.[6]

(2) We could have no awareness of ourselves as persons save out of intercourse with other minds. We do not begin with a full knowledge of ourselves, then reason by analogy to the existence of other minds like our own. Again this is to reverse the actual order. I come to believe in myself as a person because I see other people treating me as a person. We come to our earliest self-consciousness through a series of contrast effects. A child imitates the doings of

others. One of the earliest imitations is speech. The child then becomes painfully aware of the contrast between the other's way of doing and his own. This contrast is heightened when he finds purposes that conflict with his own. It is then that self-consciousness suffers a rude awakening. Even into adult life, as both Royce and James have pointed out, my consciousness of self fluctuates, borrows heavily from what others think of me, resists their blame, welcomes their praise, is heightened by the one, depressed by the other. It is doubtful if any of us could keep his sanity long if everyone else ignored us, addressed no word to us, acknowledged no question of ours, looked through and beyond but never at us, treated us as non-existent. Richard Byrd's trying experience with solitude near the South Pole is not a test case. There he knew that others were at least thinking of him. Royce claims that an infant left alone, grown to maturity without human companionship, would as an adult have about as much self-consciousness as a fairly well-educated cat.[7]

What then is this knowledge of other minds, so plainly necessary to our very existence as self-conscious subjects, yet for which no rational explanation can be found? And what is this philosophy which for generations faces this specter, yet never calls into question its own categories which are helpless in answering one of the simplest questions of experience? And what is this *scientia*, this knowledge, which scorns all that is not exact and objective, and in so doing renders itself incapable of understanding the very conditions that make its own existence possible? And what of this culture of ours which boasts of its control over nature and is skeptical of everything that cannot be brought into its physical categories? A theory of knowledge, which is helpless in the presence of so basic a knowledge as that of our neighbor's mind, has been drawn on too meager lines.

Let us have a better look at it. What really happens when we know another person? At first, our knowledge of persons is instrumental. The small child looks on his parents and his playmates as so many convenient devices for his own pleasure. When they succeed in making him feel pleasant they have his unqualified favor. When they deny his demands, or persist in doing something in their way, they arouse his anger. Yet it is in just this thwarting that he begins to recognize these people about him as subjects and not mere objects of experience. In adult life most of the people whom we meet are mere devices for our own purposes. For us the grocer, the garage mechanic, the barber, the corner policeman, our fellow employees, even the members of our own families, exist for what they mean to us, scarcely at all for what they mean to themselves. A minister is often tempted to treat people as statistics to improve his own record. This is the supreme blight of a large city—worse even than its slums—its loneliness. The people whom we meet are animated objects, little more. We have not the time, or inclination, to stop and ask ourselves about this attendant at a filling station, what it is like to be himself. What are his anxieties about his children? What is his faith? What are his hidden hopes and secret shames? We never succeed in knowing people until we know them as subjects.

Nor can we stop short of that knowledge. Early in our education we learn to respect some of the rights of other persons. We cannot endure to live in a world of hostile people. We must contrive to win some of them as allies and friends. So we are driven to seek knowledge of them as persons. What are the conditions of such knowledge?

(1) Comradeship: we must spend time with those whom we would know. Only thus can we learn their opinions and their purposes. We rely principally on conversation. As we talk I have constantly to revise my estimate of my friend. But it is when he "unburdens his heart" to me that I listen most attentively. Here I am getting at the real man. He alone can impart his meanings in full clarity. "For what person knows a man's thoughts except the spirit of the man which is in him?" [8] But he can never impart himself to

me fully, precisely because he is as much of an enigma to himself as I am to myself. If we are mature we never take another's estimate of himself at face value. We are subject to illusions about ourselves. Pride, sensitiveness, anxiety, all pervert our knowledge of ourselves. It is a needful part of our duty to each other as friends to bring these illusions to light, to be faithful in correcting our respective self-estimates.

(2) Another condition of knowing persons as subjects is a common physical world. It is a commonplace among hunters and fishermen that you never know a man until you are alone with him in the "bush." In that encounter with raw nature his conventional self dwindles and you see him more as he is. For some men it is friendship's most severe test. In less obvious ways we learn to know people in our encounter with common affairs. A stranger comes into my study, a place which is uniquely my own and where every object, every book, is a part of my private self. From the moment he enters, this small world is no longer my private world. It is his as well. He has entered into me.

But this common world is not merely physical. It is also the world of tasks to be done, of wrongs to be righted, of human needs to be met. When a common burden rests upon our shoulders, when we face a common danger, when we share a common hope that makes demands upon both of us, then I begin to know my friend as a person.

(3) We must meet other people together. This friend of mine needs to share not only my world of objects but my company of friends, if I am to know him. It is not that I am suspicious of him and must be reassured that my other friends find him trustworthy. It is that I do not know him until I see him responding to other persons. An intimacy of two, if love and integrity be in them, confers rich graces. But a world of two is too small and will inevitably dwarf its occupants. We have no interest in an empty person any more than we have in a "thing-in-itself" about which

we can know nothing. The meanings that come alive in us, our participation in the world of nature and persons, are what make us interesting to other people.

(4) Trust is another condition of knowing a person. I must believe in the integrity of a friend or I shall withhold myself from him and he will respond in kind. We shall assure each other that our friendship serves no base ends of self-interest, that we are not using each other. While this faith depends upon a growing experience, in the final stages of high friendship our knowledge of each other goes far beyond the limits of rational knowledge. A young devotee of scientific accuracy declares, "I will believe in nothing that I cannot prove." One can imagine this young man approaching the lady of his choice with a rational proposal of marriage! "My dear," he begins, "I have the hypothesis that you and I could be successfully married. But I never believe without proof. What evidence can you offer that you will be a good wife, a good manager of the home, be able to bear healthy children and care for them wisely, be interested in my work and live within my income? I shall undertake on my part to offer you whatever evidence you need to reassure you!"

(5) The supreme condition of knowing another is love. As long as we do not love, we "see through a glass darkly." We shall know "as we are fully known" only when we love. For the deepest secrets of a human person are reserved for the respect, the patience, the strength, the tenderness of love. Love is not really blind; that is a slander supported by those who do not love. Love sees what must otherwise be invisible.

In these homely and familiar experiences is the kind of knowledge upon which our very life depends. It is a knowledge which reason finds itself quite powerless to encompass. Try to imprison this knowledge in the limits of mathematical accuracy and you will destroy it. This is the hidden difficulty of our culture. But, one objects, what you call knowledge of other persons is not really knowledge: it is faith. Granted, but it is at the same time a kind of knowing. For in all our faith we are trusting people as they react to us, as they show themselves to be, as they meet their responsibilities. When we meet a new acquaintance part of us keeps hidden. What sort of person is here? Is he friend or foe? If I risk something on him what will happen to me? Is it safe to trust him? If he is humble, what secret of greatness is here? Perhaps I have found one with whom I may be sincere. This reserve disappears as friendship grows. Some of the insights of faith are the condition of larger knowledge. Indeed, faith itself creates some of the experiences upon which reason may draw in a clearer understanding of our friends.

The pathetic fact is that we never fully succeed in knowing anyone. Even our dearest ones surprise us by sudden impulses as, indeed, we surprise ourselves. There is mystery in the human soul which even the most faithful and tender lover may not penetrate. We never reveal ourselves completely in our deeds, nor in our response to nature. Ministers are often asked if we shall recognize each other in Heaven, meaning, will we know each other there as well as we do here? The question is wrongly put. Will we rather there surpass these walls of insularity and really mingle with them, soul with soul, as we never have been able to do in this life? But it is plain that we are here dealing with a kind of knowledge that involves the whole man, is fateful for our very existence, and is strangely compounded with faith.

Let us pause and review the argument. We have seen that all knowledge has both an external and an internal meaning. The external meaning is expressed through the existential reference of the judgment. In its simplest form the internal meaning is the motor response to our ideas, what we propose to do about them. In its fullest form, internal meaning is the whole complex of our purposes, from the simplest organic purposes to the most speculative and abstract. Into this internal meaning is also gathered all the relativities of our finite position as knowers. We have also seen the disastrous consequences when internal and external mean-

ing are sundered. The disaster is not apparent in the physical
sciences. Indeed, science seeks to depersonalize its symbols as the
condition of its existence. But riddles appear to plague the scientific mind. What is the nature of scientific thought which cannot
be explained by scientific categories? What of this utter dependence upon our knowledge of other persons, a knowledge which
remains inexplicable to the scientific mind? Whence the difficulties
of the social sciences in achieving accuracy and objectivity without so great a degree of abstraction as to render the results of
dubious worth? Why this demonic clash of social and economic
interests that continues to surprise and confuse everyone who puts
his trust in the rationality of man? These are some of the consequences of forgetting the place of internal meaning in all thought.
We hinted that if we could find the real basis of union of our
external and internal meaning, we should probably find the meeting place of faith and reason, as well as the source of their conflict
and the hope of their reconciliation. We said that such a discovery would prove important for the philosophy of religion.

We have seen what it means to come to a knowledge of other
persons. We have seen what commonplace and practical experiences, such as conversation and a common burden, become
the vehicle of internal meaning. Without the faith that inheres
in internal meaning we cannot even have friends, much less know
them. Two friends in their knowledge of each other depend upon
the interaction of their internal meanings, the play and counter-
play of private interest. Knowledge is possible only when our
private interests are purified. Knowledge of other persons is
ethical, reserved for men of goodwill. When our private interests
never meet, we treat each other as objects, never as persons. If
by faith we mean a personal relation of trust, respect, love, it is
obvious that there can be no knowledge of persons apart from
faith.

But it is just as plain that this faith has also its external meaning.
My friend is never a mere blank, without meaning to me. I

cannot know him by faith except as I know much about him. He is this kind of person; he thinks in this way; he holds these ethical views; he has such and such beliefs; his place in the community can be described accurately. This is our discovery: it is in personal encounter that the union of internal and external meaning is made clear. It is here that we validate our thesis, *reason and faith fulfill themselves only by working together, in full recognition of their mutual dependence.*

Nor is this a trivial discovery. Without the knowledge of other persons we should have no world of objects, no consciousness of ourselves, indeed no self at all. Any theory of knowledge, therefore, which makes incredible or irrational our knowledge of other persons, thereby demonstrates its own incompleteness. I recall a fellow student who was going through a healthy period of complete skepticism. At the same time he was very much in love with the girl whom he later married. "But," he confided, "I won't let any of my logical categories touch her!" So much the worse for his logical categories as this man has long since learned. Now note this most important conclusion: any skeptical denial that we can know God, which at the same time involves a denial of the knowledge of our fellows, we can forthwith and instantly dismiss. We may not be able to say *how* we know. If so, we clearly show that our theory of knowledge is at best partial and needs re-examination. Epistemology has left the track just so far as it has forgotten the scene of all experience, the person with his subjective interests, and the social context of persons which provides the matrix of all knowledge from the mathematical to the most intimately personal. The importance of this discovery can scarcely be exaggerated.

Now let us observe some preliminary and important consequences. If our knowledge of God bears any resemblance to our knowledge of other persons, then it is impossible to separate knowledge from faith. The attempt of some theologians to disparage the cognitive bearing of faith becomes a pretense that can scarcely be distinguished from nonsense. I cannot understand

Richard Kroner's remark,[9] "I cannot combine in one and the same act the attitude of theoretical comprehension and that of prayer or submission to the will of God and acknowledgment of his majesty." This can be true only on the narrowest understanding of the word "comprehension." The great prayers of the Church always begin with an ascription that focuses our attention upon some attribute of God, or some historical work of His. "Almighty and most merciful Father"—every word a concept including that momentous "and!" "Almighty God, *who* . . . hast built Thy Church upon the foundation of the apostles and the prophets; . . . didst endue Thine apostles with the gifts of the Holy Spirit; . . . hast made of one blood all nations of men; . . . hast given us grace at this time with one accord to make our common supplications unto Thee." Faith without comprehension is empty just as comprehension without faith is blind.

A second important consequence follows. We have seen that in the social sciences, as well as in all forms of concrete knowledge, the moral element in objectivity becomes highly important. Nor can we come to a knowledge of other persons without at the same time becoming ethically sensitive to their internal meanings. On this human level moral inadequacy is a barrier to knowledge. We should therefore expect that moral defects would prove the most serious obstacle to our knowledge of God. This is the meaning of that quaint expression which our grandfathers used, about which theologians have talked, and to which almost nobody else has paid any attention in recent years. I refer to "the noetic effect of sin." We have been discussing the limits of reason in the knowledge of God, limits that inhere in the nature of reason and in man's finitude. The Bible makes much of these limitations. They are most dramatically presented in the closing chapters of the book of Job. "Where wast thou when I laid the foundations of the earth? Declare, if thou hast understanding." [10] But this is an altogether different element, the perversion of reason by sin. The biblical utterances on this element are more veiled. St. Paul speaks of the "darkened understanding" [11] and of the natural man being unable to know the things of God.[12] The Roman Church, as we have seen, holds that the understanding of man is injured but not destroyed by sin, and that the injury is repaired by grace. This provides a ground for natural theology. The reformers, however, repudiated all human merit; salvation is by grace alone. This applies to a man's thoughts as well as to his deeds. Brunner, while holding to the natural revelation, declares that the sinner is so blinded that he cannot receive this revelation in nature until he is restored by the grace of God. It is part of his sin that he "suppresses" the truth about God.

Plainly if all this is true it is also very important. The blanket assertion that all human thinking is perverted by sin will not be given serious consideration unless the perversion is specified. It has not impressed the world of thought. Philosophers have their embarrassments, but the sinful perversion of their intellects is not one of them. The Reformed doctrine of the complete perversion of the will has had a good airing. You know what that means, whether you believe it or not. But this perversion of the intellect—what does it mean? The question has received altogether too scant attention from the theologians.

It is quite plain that as long as we define knowledge in mathematical-scientific terms the phrase has no meaning, except in the humorous supposition that mistakes in counting change are usually in your own favor. But there stands the test of objectivity. The independent observer is at hand, ready to confirm the results of your experiment. Any sin on your part will be quickly brought to light and that you well know. Moreover the child of grace need expect no special favors, no burst of illumination, in solving a problem in calculus or in making a scientific inquiry. The laws of scientific logic are strangely indifferent to the moral quality of the thinker, save in one point only, intellectual integrity. Insofar as knowledge is defined in mathematical terms, the "noetic effect of sin" is without meaning.

But when we move from the abstract to the concrete sciences, and especially to our knowledge of other persons, where internal meaning becomes determinative, then the perversion of our thinking by sin becomes disastrously clear. Let us consider some familiar instances.

As long as we are "under sin" we must suppress the truth about ourselves. We pay this tribute to the moral law, that we find our security in the pretense that we are at least decent and respectable. There is one question, which if put to any audience anywhere, will usually receive a unanimous affirmative vote. Let the audience be from any nation, class or race, they will all vote "Aye!" The only negative votes would come from morally sensitive people. The question: if all people were just as decent, honest, diligent and kind as you are, would this be a safe and decent world in which to live? But one look at our world and we know that something is wrong, somebody is the victim of pretense. The pretense becomes apparent in ourselves when our motives are questioned. We rush to our own defense, thereby demonstrating that deep within ourselves we know we need defending. Courts of law have long recognized this weakness. No man is competent to judge his own case, when his private interests are involved.

Yet this is only one aspect of the difficulty. Deep within us is a longing for perfect justice. We know that the world is incapable of any save a very crude and external kind of justice toward us. Like Job, we want to find One who knows us completely, before Whom we can present our case and be vindicated or condemned. Our constant resentment against human injustice is in itself an appeal to the divine justice. As long as the perfect judgment is withheld we cannot be secure. Of course, we dread this judgment. Herein is one of the self-contradictions of the sinner. He needs judgment and is afraid of it. So he oscillates between his proud, complacent decency and his uneasy, fearful looking for judgment.

The latter is often suppressed and deeply hidden even from a man's own awareness. But that it is never destroyed is evident from his resentment over the world's injustice to himself.

A second disastrous effect of sin upon our thinking is the perversion of our moral judgment. As long as our confidence is in our own righteousness we are under pressure to accept a moral ideal that is relative to our own performance. The man of the world will admit no need of saving, especially if the price of his salvation is the repudiation of his own decency. He pays his taxes. He takes good care of his family. He pays his employees as much as, or more than, they are worth. He supports public charities. Implicit here is a moral standard that is only slightly above his own conduct.

The same perversion of moral judgment appears in the churches. This accounts in part for the heavy emphasis upon trivial moral negatives, all of them relatively easy of attainment. While the church pays lip service to the absolute moral demands of Jesus, the actual operative moral standard in the average Protestant church, the standard by which church members judge each other, is a curious and unholy mixture of pagan morality, primitive folk ways, and bourgeois middle class respectability, seasoned by a few maxims drawn from the Bible. Even in the churches men cannot endure the white light of Jesus' high demand: complete love of God, and love for one another even as Jesus has loved us.[13] That light is too damaging to our pride to be endured.

Still another disastrous effect of sin upon human thinking is in the distortion of our judgment of our fellows. When my confidence is in my own goodness then it is painful to discover another who far exceeds me. I am driven to look for some flaw in him, take some comfort in his failures. If he ever suffers some conspicuous moral collapse I outwardly deplore his conduct. But inwardly I am relieved. The pressure is off. This particular disastrous consequence of human sin baffles the human imagination. Only God can know its awful fruitage. Love, in the New Testament meaning, "is never glad when others go wrong, love is gladdened by goodness, always slow to expose, always eager to believe the best, always hopeful, always patient." [14]

It should be observed that the work of sanctification is never so distinct from justification as the theologians often make it out to be. In the three samples which we have just described, sanctification begins in, and is a part of, justification. When a man really accepts the forgiving grace of Christ, when his confidence is no longer in his own decency but in the mercy brought to him by the Christ, then God becomes for him his "defense, rock and high tower." Then he will be prepared to know the worst about himself and the sting of resentment under criticism will be drawn. He has been humbled. He will then be prepared to look in wonder and joy upon the moral excellence of the law of Jesus. He will tend to take no delight in the failure of others. This is the very heart of the work of sanctification. Until some signs of these particular results begin to appear, no man can claim to have faith in the justification of God.

The disastrous effects of sin which we have seen in individual thinking become all the more odious and fateful in man's collective life. The perversion of judgment there becomes demonic. The righteousness of my own class and nation, its immunity to moral judgment, the perversion of moral standards when any group becomes the judge of its own case, the pleasure we ourselves take in supporting the justice of our own cause by reciting the vices of the enemy, all have been amply illustrated in recent history.[15] It is safe to say that we shall never know lasting peace on the earth until men bring their class, their labor union, their manufacturers' association, their nation, their race, their denomination under the judgment of Him who "will judge between many peoples, and will decide concerning strong nations afar off." [16] [17]

This evidence of the perversion of thought by sin in our human relations should prepare us to understand in part how disastrous is the same corruption in our knowledge of God. If we accept the biblical estimate of sin, that it consists of man's usurping the place of God, then we shall be prepared to find fatal damage to human thinking whenever man's vital interests are involved. In so far as human thought proceeds on the assumption of man's selfsufficiency apart from God, that man can discover his own meaning, determine his own truth, pose and answer his own questions, then the whole course of modern secular thought is a huge example of the perversion of reason by sin. How it has perverted his own thought no man is wise enough to say. It follows that he has no right to use this principle as an easy explanation of "unsound" doctrine in others. Occasionally a thinker is as candid as Mr. Aldous Huxley when he writes, "I had motives for not wanting the world to have a meaning; consequently assumed that it had none, and was able without any difficulty to find satisfying reasons for this assumption." [18]

This tendency to suppress the limitations of our finite perspective has been characteristic of most idealism from Hegel to the present. Idealism deifies reason and so comes to a superficial and premature identification of human reason with the mind of God. Idealism at the same time obscures the distinction between God and man, the Creator and the created. It is not therefore prepared to recognize the sinful corruption of reason because of man's inability to accept the humble status of creature, his inability to recognize that his judgment is limited by his place in nature, in history, and his location in groups, such as nation, class, race and denomination. Indeed, idealism talks more of evil than it does of sin and is forced by its inner logic to underestimate evil, and even to make it essential to the harmony of the Absolute. Our finite reason, for the idealists and all who have come under their influence, thus suffers from the sinful pretension that it is divine, identical with the reason of God.

Practically every sinner does an even more brash thing: he replaces the eternal meaning with his own fragmentary pulse of meaning as though he himself were God! When man thus claims the place of God, there is bound to appear in his thinking a hostility toward God, an almost frantic attempt to hold some citadel of human pride and sufficiency against the claims of God. Man's self-security predisposes him to accept a view of life which excludes God. We settle many questions, ease many burdens, escape many responsibilities if God can be banished. Or finding that road too difficult, we can travel the road of idealism and have a God that we do not confront, except as the logical extension of our own thought. But to confront the God who has revealed Himself in history, and at a point of time two thousand years ago, among a people who knew not our science, cared not for our philosophy, this is quite too humiliating to be borne! This revelation implies our helplessness, the bankruptcy of our virtue and of our reason. Our resentment at this revelation is perhaps the supreme illustration of how sin perverts human thought.

But is the perversion complete? I cannot believe so. Man is unable to live with the pretense that all is well. He is aware to some extent of self-contradiction within himself, and of disaster in his world. Man as sinner is by no means incapable of discerning the judgment of God upon himself and upon his world. There is deep within him some longing that God will speak. This is the "connecting point" for divine grace. His pride is not insuperable. Suppress our fears and misgivings as we will, we can never escape them entirely. Nor are we utterly unable to understand God when He speaks, especially if He will speak in compassion and *to our need*.

CHAPTER 7

Revelation and Faith

The analogy between our knowledge of God and our knowledge of other persons is by no means complete. Our knowledge of God *may* be more intimate, more primary, more essential than is our knowledge of human persons. I am inclined to think that we look too far for our knowledge of God, searching the starry heavens, the beginning of things, and ancient records, when there is a word of God that is very near to us, not only in our speech but in our thought, in our very existence; that God is the condition of every thought, the hidden major premise of every syllogism; that, as Hocking said, it is the knowledge of God that makes possible our knowledge of nature and our knowledge of other persons; that it is this knowledge of God that makes us restless with any finite stopping place for our inquiries; that it is this knowledge of God that forever makes the rebel against God uncomfortable and homeless; that it is this knowledge of God which makes it possible for God to reveal himself to us. I am not concerned to offer proof of this hidden knowledge. It is as yet a private conviction that we have here a possibly fruitful hypothesis. Nor am I dissuaded in this conviction because it is a hidden knowledge. Our knowledge of other persons is for the most part hidden. We are seldom aware that even in our most private meditations we are not alone. Others invade our privacy. An Other is also there. Such hidden knowledge is not useful for faith until it is brought to light, just as our implicit knowledge of other persons provides us with no friends, gives us no loved ones. To bring this hidden knowledge to full awareness is our greatest concern.

Consider, then, how you have come to such *explicit* knowledge of God as you now have. If you were brought up in a Christian home, you heard your parents pray. You early felt their authority over you, often in a painful way. But you came to respect their authority when you learned, as John Baillie has put it, that they were under the same authority themselves. They, as well as you, were bound by some One. At this stage you felt the presence of God rather than knew Him.

You heard older people talk to Him and about Him. You began presently to make your own prayers and to read your Bible. You heard that He was the Creator of all things, that He was Lord over all His creatures, that your very life depended upon His care, that as your Judge He condemned your sin and that as your loving Savior He would forgive your sins.

As you grew older you began your study of science. As the cozy world of your childhood gave way to the terrifying vastness of your adult world, skeptical doubts came to you. You studied philosophy; you read about proofs of God's existence; you read your Bible with new intensity; and you read theology. Yet you had not attained to a knowledge of God.

But one day, perhaps fairly early in life, you encountered Him. Here again the analogy of our knowledge of human friends fails. For this encounter with God was a far more momentous kind of knowledge. Here was One who knew you far better than you knew yourself, who knew your secret parts "when as yet there was none of them." [1] All of you was present in that encounter: body and soul, thought, feeling, purpose, faith, your sins and your hopes, your past as well as your present. You became a real individual in that moment. Philosophy, theology, tradition, authority, your own restless longing, all these may have helped to bring you there. But there was also something fatefully different. You said "Thou" and "I." In the presence of that "Thou" your "I" was more of a person than ever before. Yet even here you remembered something of what you had learned from authority and experience. You were not alone with God. Your parents, your teachers, the prophets, the Apostles were there and most of all the Man from Nazareth. What happened?

I have referred to this intimate personal experience because this is exactly the issue of revelation. A revelation in a church or in a book to someone else is only a potential revelation. It is in the personal encounter that revelation is fulfilled.

Let us first be quite clear about the need of revelation. Many thoughtful men resist the very idea of revelation as primitive mythology. They have much justification for their doubt. Revelation has often been presented as a miraculous imparting of an imposing body of facts. These facts are usually of a sort that man could have discovered for himself, given sufficient time and the willingness to follow the scientific method. Yet to question any of these "facts" was supposed to be an affront against God. A careful study of the Bible ought to make clear how inept is this whole concept of revelation. It may be seriously questioned whether any facts were imparted, if we mean facts capable of scientific verification.

But if God is the supreme subject of experience, then He alone can declare His own meaning, His own purpose. And if our life and death interest is in our relation to Him, then what God has to say about that relation is of first importance. Paul gave the final argument for revelation, "For what person knows a man's thoughts except the spirit of the man which is in him? So also no one comprehends the thoughts of God except the Spirit of God." [2] If God is really God, then all that men think about Him, all that we can experience, all our reasons and "surmises of faith" are unimportant and irrelevant before what God has to say about Himself.

There are three life and death questions which we cannot answer for ourselves, where our thought and our experience are dumb. Denied any word from God, we are doomed to ignorance of a very fateful kind.

The first question concerns the being of God Himself. The

biblical answer is that God is alone God, that He is the Creator. Now this is beyond our thought. We can use the words "creation out of nothing," but we cannot think them. We cannot even imagine what they mean. Even our imagination partakes of the form of time and we are quite powerless to conceive a beginning in time. We ask, what was before the beginning? A first cause we can dimly imagine, but a first cause itself in time. But the Creator of space and time, and of all things in them, this is beyond our thought. Yet it is utterly essential if God really be God. He alone *is*. All else has contingent being. This rational contradiction is so severe that recent thinkers have tried to escape it by resort to a finite God, a God of pure purpose who is trying to mold a recalcitrant world to His will.[3] Yet such a God is at best a candidate for Godhead. But if God Himself speaks to us, assures us that He is, the first life and death question has its only possible answer.

The second vital question concerns our destiny and our death. Let us be clear about the question. It is not merely our own survival after death. Most of us, I suppose, could muster enough heroism to give up life, however much we loved being alive, and however clearly we understood that death meant extinction, *if some good came of it*. But death is far more devastating. It is the negation not only of life but of all for which we live. All our loves, all our loyalties, all the human beings that give meaning to all our institutions, all for which we labor and love and hope, all are under sentence of death. It is against this universal destruction that man has been in revolt.

For this question our human reason is inadequate. Plato's argument from the indissolubility of the soul [4] is not convincing in the light of modern psychoanalysis. It is not inconceivable that mind or spirit should survive the death of the body. Reason has at least established this as a possibility. Yet we cannot even imagine it. Our position in space, the world of objects about us, our kinaesthetic and visceral sensations are a substantial core of our present experience. Indeed, behind much of our desire for immortality there is a covert longing for more of this life. In his play *Our Town*, Thornton Wilder makes Emily, the young wife and mother, come back again to life. She chooses as the day to live over again her twelfth birthday. When the day is over and she is about to return to the grave she cries out,

"Goodbye, world! . . . Goodbye, Grover's Corners. . . . mama and papa. . . . Goodbye to clocks ticking . . . and mama's sunflowers . . . and food and coffee and new-ironed dresses and hot baths . . . and sleeping and waking up! . . . Oh, earth, you're too wonderful for anyone to realize you!" [5]

Food and coffee, new-ironed dresses and hot baths, this is the stuff of life as we know it.

We may reason from the fact of our human love, from the threat of complete destruction without immortality, from the complete absence of meaning if death ends all, or from any of the familiar grounds that are usually advanced on Easter Sunday as reasons for immortality. Yet these arguments are but eloquent expressions of our need, of our desire, of our cry for light. They do not answer the central question: is it true? Here, to be honest, no human word will do. But if God has spoken in the Risen Christ, is that not a convincing answer? Believers innumerable have found it so.

Yet to many people this answer of the Risen Christ is not convincing. Nor does the word about Creation carry any meaning. Why not? Primarily because these are still theoretical answers. They do not sufficiently involve our internal meaning. They are therefore abstract, and in some circumstances even uninteresting. Here there is a clear analogy between our knowledge of persons and our knowledge of God. What we hear or read about other persons is abstract until our vital interests are in some way involved in that knowledge. In much the same way, there can be no knowledge of God until we ourselves are involved. It must be the whole man that enters this encounter, all his internal meaning, every vital interest, as well as every bit of his external meaning.

This is why we can never find a convincing answer to the questions about creation and death until we find an answer to the third question.

What then is this third and most important life and death question? It is this: what is God's attitude toward us as sinners? The question of sin is the basic question of Christian faith. It is safe to say that the survival of Christianity itself depends upon the validity of the biblical diagnosis of the human predicament. The correctness of this diagnosis will never be settled by reasoned argument. It has been, is being, and will be confirmed in private experience and in the demonic clash of social interests.

Had Kant confronted this third question, his answer to our first two questions would have been entirely different. But as long as we accept a merely moralistic conception of sin, as the disregard of this or that human custom, or even as the breaking of this or that divine commandment, we cannot understand our sin, or the need of a revelation, or the meaning of God's forgiveness. If breaking law is the essence of sin, then all the Pelagian answers to the question of sin are right. If this or that vicious habit is the only meaning of human disability, then man can save himself. We have known men who under some deep emotional strain have made a break with old habit. If righteousness before God is only moralism, then Kant and Macintosh are right in their doctrine of forgiveness. When a man breaks with an old habit, and starts a new life, neither God nor man should hold the old sin against him. We should give him a new chance and do all in our power to help him succeed.

But the biblical teaching on sin is far more profound. Sin is basically revolt against God. It is pride. It is disobedience. It is idolatry, substituting ourselves for God, taking to ourselves the prerogative over our own life and the lives of others that belongs to God alone. It is the arrogant assumption that our private, limited perspective ought to be the perspective of all other people and of God Himself. It is anxiety over our humble position as creatures who are dependent upon God for our very being, for wisdom, for safety. The voice of the tempter always suggests, "Ye shall be as gods." [6] All other sins flow from this basic sin. The psychological principle of compensation illuminates this biblical doctrine. Bitterness and hatred—they reveal to the discerning mind that a man does not like himself. Fear—what is it but Kierkegaard's "dizziness of freedom"? Greed and injustice—what are they save man's pathetic barricade against dangers supposed to be without? Violence and war—what are they save the whole sorry mass of human fear rolled up into a demonic weight of cruelty and destruction?

It should be clear that we cannot really understand what sin is until God has revealed Himself to us in His saving grace. Only in the perspective of forgiving grace are we honest enough to see the vicious perversion of our own perspective, and how it has subtly corrupted every human relation, every word, every deed, every thought. Penitence on its intellectual side is the recognition of the pride of finite perspective. All men have some knowledge of sin. We can clearly recognize it in others. We may even have some misgivings about it in ourselves and bravely undertake its correction. But we cannot see it clearly except in penitence. Nor is penitence possible without at least the first beginnings of confidence in the divine mercy.

If all this is true, then we are utterly dependent upon revelation for this, the central concern of the human spirit. Man cannot remove his own alienation from God. This hostility has become a part of his very being. Plainly we cannot forgive ourselves. Nor can any man pronounce our forgiveness. If we reason our way into forgiveness, or if we demand it as our own right, we thereby demonstrate that we have not confronted the meaning of sin. We have no natural right even to pray for forgiveness. Even that right and that hope are conferred on us only when God Himself declares His merciful attitude toward us as sinners.

Moreover, this declaration must be in a morally convincing event. A human forgiveness that casually brushes aside the past sin, answers no need, heals no wounds, forgives no sins. Even human love suffers in forgiveness, the more so just because the forgiveness is gladly bestowed and lovingly imparted. So the perfect love of God must suffer. This is the profound truth in all "objective" theories of the atonement. "Moral influence" there is in all forgiveness and it is powerful. But if forgiveness is the mere change in our subjective attitudes, it is not enough. The forgiveness simply will not hold fast. If we accept forgiveness in faith, it is only because God Himself is "just *and* the justifier of him that hath faith in Jesus." [7] The New Testament teaching is clear: this objective revelation took place in the death of Jesus Christ, the Son of God. There alone did God make clear His mercy toward sinful man.

This is the basic revelation. When by faith a man accepts this revelation, he is not receiving a divine body of facts. He himself is being made a "new creature." His center is being restored to where it belonged all along, in God. God becomes God again. Man is man once more. In consequence, man is able to understand himself, his world, his fellow man, his real destiny. No reasoned argument of sinful man could ever produce this change. No man can do it for himself. That is why revelation and salvation are *phases of one event*. There can be no knowledge of God through revelation apart from saving faith in God. It is precisely in this knowledge that we are prepared to believe that God is Creator, and that God, having raised us from the death of sin, has already imparted eternal life to us.

What has this revelation in Jesus Christ to do with the Bible? The Bible, as Martin Luther said, is the cradle in which Christ is laid. There is revelation in the Old Testament. But the revelation, it is essential to note, is *in* events *and in* the prophetic interpretation of those events. By themselves the events might mean anything, and they did. The complaint of the prophets is that God has done much for Israel, but the people, being ungrateful, did not see the goodness of God in the events. "I have nourished and brought up children, and they have rebelled against me." [8] This is the characteristic cry of the prophets. Yet the prophets declared God through the event, through the goodness of past mercies, through the rigors of present judgment, through the hope that could yet be fulfilled. The prophets pointed beyond themselves. They were like the good teacher who seeks to make himself no longer necessary to the pupil. The Old Testament reveals both the judgment and the forbearance of God. Yet it is not complete. Nor was the Old Testament system of sacrifice complete.

The aim of sacrifice was to abolish the separation between God and man, and to introduce the Presence, the dwelling of God among men. Neither was possible; the cultus merely suggested something which *ought* to happen. It was, so to speak, an unfulfilled postulate, and one which could not be fulfilled.[9]

But in Jesus Christ something radically new appears. He does not point men beyond himself, he calls them to himself. "Come to me, all who labor and are heavy-laden, and I will give you rest." [10] Here, indeed, is One who is "more than a prophet." Here is a standard of righteousness more sublime and unattainable than any ever enunciated in the Old Testament. Here is judgment more awesome than any ever pronounced by prophet of old. Here is mercy clearer and more persuasive. And in the death of Christ, God reveals both the dimensions of human sin and the abundance of His grace. In the writings of the Apostles we begin to see clearly what the early church found in Jesus Christ. They, too, are an indispensable part of the revelation.

It should be obvious that this is the kind of revelation that is "once for all." It is not the kind of revelation that yields to Hocking's "postulate" that

in whatever way God has been known and heard by any of the prophets, or by seers of more ancient date . . . in fundamentally that same manner is God known by all God-knowing men at all times.[11]

This revelation is not repeatable. Nor can the Christ who is the Word of God be reduced to Macintosh's proportions as the su-

preme example of "right religious adjustment," or to a pattern
that we can more or less approximate. Modern man objects that
this revelation should have been made so long ago, or that it should
have been withheld so long. He objects that it was made among
the Jews, rather than among the more cultivated Greeks. But if
God was to do the revealing, and if our very destiny hangs on
that revelation, then it behooves us to be more humble and to ask
the factual question: where *has* the revelation actually taken place?

Since revelation is personal encounter, the revelation in Jesus
Christ is not revelation for any man until he receives it by faith.
In this sense of the word Hocking and Macintosh were profoundly
right. We are on the same level at this point with the apostles.
Until I can say, "My Lord and My God," the revelation is dark and
foreign to me. It is only when I renounce my own precarious
security, quit trusting in my own righteousness, that I am ready
to receive Jesus Christ as my Savior and as the Word of God to me.
Only then can I speak of him "who loved me and gave himself
for me." [12] It is only then that God becomes the center of life, only
then that the blindness of sin is healed. Faith *is* the knowledge of
God, the only kind of knowledge that is possible for the sinner
who has been in revolt against God. It is only in this saving encounter that faith and reason, internal and external meaning, come
to their fulfillment, as well as to their provisional harmony with
each other.

But the New Testament writers were so convinced of the subtle
dangers of human pride that they would not regard even their
faith as their own doing. A faith which lets the sinner observe how
strong is his confidence is simply not faith, but a very subtle and
dangerous form of human pride. New Testament faith is the looking away from self to Jesus Christ. Our faith is *in* him or it is not
faith. Accordingly, the New Testament and the Church have
taught that saving faith is the work of the Holy Spirit; that without this renewal we could not even believe. It follows that the
faith by which we receive the forgiveness of sins and the faith by

which we receive the revelation of God in Christ, are one faith. Likewise, the assurance that we are forgiven and that the revelation in Christ is indeed the Word of God, are one working of the Holy Spirit.

This is the profound truth in the New Testament teaching that only those who believe, know; that "if any man's will is to do his will, he shall know"; [13] that God has hidden "these things from the wise and understanding and revealed them to babes"; [14] that preaching must not be "with eloquent wisdom, lest the cross of Christ be emptied of its power"; [15] that "since, in the wisdom of God, the world did not know God through wisdom, it pleased God through the folly of what we preach to save those who believe"; [16] that "the wisdom of this world is folly with God." [17] This is the full truth of which Kant had caught a partial glimpse when he wrote, "If you do not take care that you first make men at least moderately good, you will never make them honest believers." [18] All this seems like arguing in a circle. One recent volume puts it:

How do we know anything about God or even know there is a God when all human powers of knowledge are incapable of reaching to God? We know because God reveals himself to those whom he may choose. But how do we know what is God's revelation and what is not? God himself will cause us to know. There is nothing more to say about it.[19]

Yet if we accept the biblical estimate of sin, if we take seriously the havoc wrought by human sin, if we put all our faith in God, that is all we shall want to have said about it. Faith and revelation are organic aspects of the personal encounter where man as penitent sinner meets the God of forgiving mercy.

When we see faith and revelation related in this way, we are prepared to remove some recent misunderstanding as to what both faith and revelation are. Faith is commonly regarded as an inferior kind of information, which will one day be replaced by direct knowledge. Faith is doggedly holding to a rational proposition, for which the objective evidence is always represented by a low fraction of probability. It is a kind of crutch which the crippled man uses only until returning strength enables him to throw it away. But saving and revealing faith in Christ is not directed to a proposition, whatever its fraction of probability. It is not so much belief in what is said as trust in Him who speaks. Faith and knowledge can never be severed without destroying both of them. The attempt to direct faith toward a rational content, equating it with belief, has obscured the central meaning of faith in the New Testament.

Again, faith is often taken as the "will to believe." It confronts the ambiguities of its world and creates its certainties out of its own valor. Such faith is commonly described by preachers as a "venture." They summon their lethargic congregations to heroic defiance of the dark facts of their world. In this same mood,

The coward within us asks for the proof; cries out that the venture is not *safe,* and summoning the will-to-disbelieve has no difficulty in finding reasons for rejecting the invitation. The hero, on the contrary, finds in the terms offered the exact conditions to which his nature is fitted to respond. He would rather *create* the proof by his own valour than have it for nothing from the outset. He is not dismayed at finding himself in a universe which puts him under no *compulsion* to believe in God, Freedom, Duty and Immortality. As a free soul he prefers not to be *compelled* to believe in anything—for how then could he be free? [20]

Faith has its heroic valor. But saving faith is not impressed with its own heroism. "Beware of wanting to make a hero out of Luther. Luther himself never felt like one." [21] Faith is a venture—of everything: of its own proud security, its own righteousness. The man of faith renounces his proud and pretentious claims to the throne of God. He stakes everything upon God. Yet such a man does not add in an undertone, "How brave am I!" His faith has been called forth by the grace of the Lord Jesus. Hence the constant comment of all his moral striving is "How good is God!" The call to faith is not to the heroic and to the defiant, but to the weary, the heavy-laden, the broken, yes, to the cowardly. Faith is not a boastful defiance of contrary fact. It is the humble acknowledgement of fulfilling and saving truth. It does not live in daily fear that its valor may be spent in the wrong direction. It is glad and confident. Faith is not proud of itself. It boasts of the grace of Jesus Christ. Such faith, we repeat, has amply manifested its heroism and that in very recent times.

Revelation has also been misrepresented as the imparting of a body of facts. Now facts at this level are highly abstract. When Christian thinkers have made the Bible a revealed array of fact on the one hand, and on the other have insisted that no one can understand this revelation without the inward illumination of the Holy Spirit, they have stated their case badly. The revelation is God's answer to the life and death question of His relation to man. It becomes the Truth, illuminating and transforming all truths. And truths are imparted in a personal encounter as though they were incidental to the main business, the restoration of man to God and of man to himself. The truth that Jesus Christ rose from the dead is of a different order from the fact that water boils at one hundred degrees Centigrade at sea level.

God has not imparted all the secrets of His nature. He has committed to no earthly authority the full knowledge of His being as He is in Himself. Vast mysteries remain and are likely to remain. Why God created the most distant star; what purpose He sees in parasites, or in long-extinct species; what is the meaning of the death of a little child; what is the inner meaning of the Atonement; these and a host of other questions are mysteries beyond our imagining. But He has revealed and imparted Himself where it is of vital importance that we know Him, in His attitude toward man as sinner. He has declared His judgment against sin and His saving purpose for the sinner in Jesus Christ. This, we repeat, is the heart of revelation. From this theologians can and have reasoned to other attributes of God. But revelation is limited to that which "is necessary for our salvation."

Nor is the Bible a body of scientific knowledge to spare us the painful inquiry of the laboratory. The attempts of biblicists to refute the findings of science by quoting texts of scripture succeed only in making the biblicists ridiculous and the Bible meaningless to vast numbers of men who desperately need its message. Nor does the Bible contain an accurate history of the life of Israel or even of the life of Jesus. The Bible is often annoying in its carelessness of historical and biographical detail. It was not written for the convenience of later historians. Its writers had more urgent business at hand.

Nor does the Bible confront us with a system of doctrine. It might have saved many controversies and many disgraceful wounds to the "body of Christ" had it done so. There seems to be an almost deliberate conspiracy among the writers of the Bible at this point. It is as though they were saying to us, "A system of doctrine would be your possession. You would make an idol of it and give to it the devotion that belongs to God alone. You shall not use our texts for the perversion of faith." The Bible presents us with the law, the prophets, the apostles, and Jesus Christ. It calls for our faith, that we may be restored to God and so recover our lost humanity.

That the Church has seldom followed the Bible at this point is one of the darkest tragedies of Christian history. The Church in its early years was compelled to formulate its doctrine in answer to the criticisms of the pagan world. These formulations are of great value today. A non-doctrinal Christianity would soon have become invertebrate and powerless. The failure to be concerned about doctrine today is simple and complete evidence of a lack of vigorous Christian faith. But there is a wide difference between Christian faith and belief in doctrine. The Roman Catholics made a fateful error at that point. It was for this reason that faith has never been regarded by Roman theologians as sufficient for salvation. It must be completed by love.

But the Protestant Church has made a similar mistake. The Reformers rightly protested the Roman system of dogma as the object of faith. They recovered the New Testament meaning of faith as a personal trust in Jesus Christ as the Word of God. All is of grace! It is true that Calvin did at times treat the Scriptures as the *ipsissima verba* of God. But he kept that belief in subjection to saving faith in Christ. The Protestant churches, as Brunner has recently said, cannot lay claim to "dogma." Their doctrinal formularies are "Confessions," confessions of their faith. It never occurred to them to make belief in the confessions a condition of salvation. But before long the emphasis of the Reformers was reversed. Belief in the authority of Scripture was held to be of primary importance. "The Scriptures are the very Word of God. God Himself cannot be the author of falsehood. Therefore, every word in the Scriptures is true." So ran their syllogism. The results have been disastrous. The pitiless light of scientific criticism has been thrown upon the Bible. The result has been, on the one hand, a sophistical defense of biblical inerrancy in a vast expenditure of fruitless energy. On the other hand, large sections of the population have lost faith in the Bible, simply because they could not honestly accept the only view of it that was offered them by their churches.

The time has come for the churches to bring this whole question into the open. Too long have church leaders followed a policy of timid evasion. Scholars who know better are afraid to say so in public. Thus, many a student regards himself as the victim of biblical criticism. He secretly envies the orthodox for their greater assurance. Yet he feels compelled by truth to what he regards as the impoverishing of his faith. He occupies a precarious position indeed! For his sake the conspiracy of silence should be broken. Furthermore nothing is to be gained by a toleration of "orthodoxy" on the ground that it is better not to "disturb the faith" of people who are unacquainted with critical questions. For if we

see clearly, it is the very threat to faith which is the principal
danger of the "orthodox" view of the Bible. This "orthodox" view
has three fatal defects.

1. It is simply not true. Inspiration is defined as the guidance
by the Holy Spirit of the writers of the Holy Scriptures, so as to
preserve them from error of every sort. This universal negative
is a fearfully insecure position for faith to occupy. The discovery
of one error—and the whole theory of inspiration is gone! It
should be clear that the Bible makes no such claim for itself. If
men were to study the Bible reverently and humbly, using the
aids of biblical research, they could arrive at no such conclusion.
The view of verbal inerrancy is a man-made doctrine, imposed
on the Bible from without. In order to evade the imposing array
of errors in the Bible, the defenders of this view are driven to
highly sophistical extremes. Thus I remember hearing one man
applying the doctrine of inspiration to Stephen's defense as contained in *The Acts*, chapter 7. This inspiration, he explained, did
not mean that all the historical references made by Stephen were
accurate. That were too great a strain on faith! It meant only that
the account of Stephen's speech was free from all error; it was
an accurate transcript of what Stephen actually said. We say
"was," for the safeguarding from error applied only to the first
manuscript written by the author of *The Acts*. That manuscript
is long since lost. We have only copies of copies of copies. Since
there are disagreements in the texts of these copies, it is plain that
the Holy Spirit did not undertake to safeguard the copies from
error, a singular oversight if the Spirit regarded inerrancy as of
such vital concern! Devout and reverent scholarship does not
prescribe to the Eternal the mode of revelation. It embodies an
objective, factual temper. It seeks to discover how God has actually
revealed Himself.

2. "Orthodox" biblicism is a very subtle and dangerous form
of idolatry. Saving faith relies upon God, and the very act of faith
is at the same time the instrument through which we receive the

revelation. The New Testament and the Reformers were clear that knowledge of God's truth is the fruit of the Spirit in the minds of those who believe. But when men regard the Bible as an inerrant system of divine truth it then becomes detached from God. It can be studied "inductively" as the orthodox theologians used to say, and binding inferences can be drawn. A man can then possess the truth quite apart from any personal encounter with God. The Protestant doctrine of *sola gratia, sola fides,* is betrayed and we are back with the Roman position that faith means the acceptance of a system of doctrine. Men thus lay claim to a certainty that is not of faith, and which is largely independent of the work of the Holy Spirit. Men thus tend to worship the Bible, and their own system of doctrine, rather than God. So subtle is this idolatry, that it is safe to say that no bibliolater will recognize that he is also an idolater.

When I go into a department store and make a purchase, the clerk wraps it up in a neat package and ties it with a string. I then walk out of the store with the package under my arm. This is what happens to the Bible-idolater. He gets his theological package neatly tied, and proceeds to walk off with it. But you cannot do that with the truth of God. It is not yours by right. Such truth as has been afforded you is the saving truth of God's mercy toward you as a sinner and all that is necessary for your salvation. It is dependable, final, authoritative. It is God's truth. But it is not a full system that gives you easy access to all the secrets of God's being, of the mysteries of time and eternity, over which less fortunate souls must struggle in doubt and uncertainty.

3. This doctrine of inerrancy confers on the Church a false and pretentious authority over the minds of men. By reason of its corporate nature, the Church has some authority over the individual. Its "confessions" are the collective witness of the denomination and serve as a corrective against the facile aberrations of individual members of the church. Yet these confessions, in most Protestant churches, are not binding upon the laity. Sub-

scription to the confession is seldom made a condition of membership. In this the churches recognize that finite perspectives are contained in their doctrine and that the doctrine is subject to new formulation with the growth of experience and insight.

Yet the churches have often forsaken this partial authority and claimed final authority over the minds of men. Religious fanaticism, the bitterness of theological controversy, religious wars, persecution, the violence of heresy hunters, the resistance to scientific discovery, the alienation of multitudes of thoughtful persons from the Church, these are some of the vicious results of this proud and sinful pretension to possessing the truth.

This arrogance of mind is in fact a denial of the faith that renounces its own righteousness before God and depends solely upon the grace of Jesus Christ. Pride of opinion is of one piece with pride in our own righteousness.

Our toleration of truths opposed to those which we confess is an expression of the spirit of forgiveness in the realm of culture. Like all forgiveness, it is possible only if we are not too sure of our own virtue.[22]

The position of uncertainty is intellectually precarious in precisely the same sense that salvation by faith is morally precarious. To the man who focuses attention upon himself, both positions are untenable. But to the man whose faith is in Jesus Christ, the one is no more cause for fear than the other. By his very faith he recognizes his own finitude and sin. He does not aspire to certainties that belong to God alone, any more than he pretends to a righteousness that is not yet his. He is content to let God be God, indeed.

The Bible is the supremely precious book to all men of faith. It contains much that is human and partial. Except under the exigencies of controversy, no man of faith would think of putting every passage in the Bible upon a level. Yet God speaks to us in the law, in the Levitical code, in the prophets, in drama and psalms. But supremely and clearly His Word is in Jesus Christ. It is not an easy wisdom for the idle and casual thinker. It is a

Word that demands from us not only thought, but faith, life, the new birth. In God's righteousness is the hope of salvation which we receive by faith. In God's truth is our light, which we receive by faith. The Holy Spirit confers on us this unitary faith, this single grace, by which we receive our salvation and our knowledge of God. We submit this as the New Testament doctrine of revelation and faith.

CHAPTER 8

Revelation and Reason

It may now seem that the philosopher has no place in the household of faith. Revelation claims supremacy. Theology is now responsible for the truth about God, about man, and concerning human destiny. Must philosophy then renounce all claims to deal with ultimate questions and give up its interest in religion? Is its work to be limited to an analysis of scientific methods and to relating the sciences so that a unified scientific view will emerge? It is to this role that Barth assigns philosophy. A large group of contemporary philosophers are quite content with this assignment. But they return Barth's compliment by consigning all that he stands for to the realm of the meaningless.

Consider the limitations that we have found in reason. We have seen that even under the impulse of Christian faith, reason has been unable to produce a single argument for the existence of God that carries conviction for all men. Much less has it been able to bring us to personal encounter with God. It cannot answer the three life and death questions of creation, the forgiveness of sins, and the life after death. In personal encounter it is vitiated by sin. Its pride and its power must be surrendered in the act of faith. Unamuno's "suffocation of spirit" and "vital anguish," when replaced by the joy and peace of faith, are not likely to find much use for reason. Faith now rests upon the Word of God. Where is the wisdom of man? It is foolishness with God. Apparently, philosophy's day is done, as far as the courts of the temple are concerned.

But this conclusion is premature and disastrous. The act of

saving faith does not obliterate the distinction between God and man. Faith repudiates the suggestion of mysticism that the individual must be lost in the Absolute. To say that all is of grace does not obliterate man; it restores him to his true stature. The man of faith is rational, perhaps for the first time. The pride of his finite perspective has been slain in principle, and he is prepared to be objective in the fullest sense. Idolatry of self, the great barrier to objectivity, has been broken in him. Christian love now requires him to recognize that other people also have their internal meaning, their purposes to be fulfilled or denied.

Moreover, he still confronts questions where reason must guide him. Let him overlook the service of reason to faith and his faith is at once vitiated by pretense and ends by becoming fanaticism. Just as internal meaning must refer to external meaning, so faith, which is a pure instance of internal meaning, is directed to the most completely objective content which the mind of man encounters. Reason pervades all experience. It enters silently into every conversation; its work appears in every meaning. It is quite willing to be anonymous, to live for the time in art, in symbol, in music, and in poetry. No emotion, however intense, excludes reason. Whenever experience refers to the real, there reason is at work. When faith apprehends God its meaning is definite. But no meaning can be definite until it is related to other truths and meanings, and this is the work of reason. Faith is based on the fact that in salvation God has communicated some of His meaning to man. His Word has been spoken. But a word that has no meaning to the hearer is no word, even though it be God's Word to man. Nor does God destroy man and replace him by an instantaneous creation capable of responding to the Word in faith.

Only the requirements of theory can lead to such an extreme. The natural man is at least capable of recognizing his need, or that he has needs even when he cannot understand them. The non-Christian religions are based upon this sense of need. All seek salvation of some sort. Man is not able to find rest of spirit without God. He cannot know the peace that passes understanding apart from faith. But he can and does long for it.

Among the needs commonly recognized in the religions of mankind we mention six. (1) With all his pretense of self-sufficiency, man knows that he depends upon a power not his own. Let the elaborate procession of the gods bear witness. By himself he is insecure. (2) He longs for a clear judgment that will be fair in estimating him, even at the risk of condemning him. He is satisfied neither with his own, nor with his fellows' judgment of himself. Again, we call as witness all the parables of judgment of the world's religions. (3) He knows that he is in contradiction with himself. The fragmentary purpose of today is at war with that of yesterday. His will is not united. He knows that he tries to reign and cannot even govern himself. (4) He is beset by fears of all kinds. He is afraid of his future, afraid of his enemies, afraid of disease, afraid of disaster, afraid of loneliness, afraid of people, afraid of his own freedom. (5) He knows that death is coming to him and that its destruction will envelop all that he holds dear, all that he has labored to establish, all that has won his loyalty. Again, we have only to recall the varying forms of immortality which the world's religions have offered and the persistence of the theme of death in the world's best literature. (6) "If you will not know God in His mercy, you will know Him in His wrath." Even this is a kind of knowledge of God. All the burden of the restlessness of the human spirit cries out for God. With these needs all preaching of the Gospel will itself be burdened, if it is touched with the compassion of Jesus. It is obvious that some knowledge of human need is quite independent of the historical revelation in Jesus Christ. Without a sense of need God's message would have no appeal to man. Nothing is so unconvincing as the answer to a question that has not been asked.

The Bible is unaware of Barth's claim that the natural man cannot hear the Word of God. Consider the patience, the variety, the grace of the speech of God to man. He appeals to historical fact. "I am Jehovah thy God, who brought thee out of the land of Egypt, out of the house of bondage." [1] This disaster, this sin, this deliverance, this judgment—all are made the vehicle of God's appeal. God's Word reaches man. The method varies. Now the appeal is to judgment:

"Why will ye be still stricken, that ye revolt more and more? the whole head is sick, and the whole heart faint. From the sole of the foot even unto the head there is no soundness in it; but wounds, and bruises, and fresh stripes. . . . Your country is desolate; your cities are burned with fire; your land, strangers devour it in your presence." [2]

Now the appeal is to gratitude as in Isaiah's parable of the vineyard.[3] Now the cry is that of a tender lover. Hosea likens God to the lover who will use all the arts of courtship to win his beloved. "I will allure her." [4] How full of grace and compassion is the Word of God! He speaks a language that we can understand.

What shall we make of the teaching method of Jesus? He took the commonplaces of man's daily life, the sower, the growing crops, a woman baking bread, the unemployed in the marketplace, the willful son who forsook home for the far country, and he made them the vehicles of eternal truth. He was not concerned that his truth should float in the air, above the heads of men, pure and uncontaminated. He wanted it to live in the affairs of men. There were times when he spoke with the dignity of Mt. Sinai as when he said, "Verily, verily, I say unto you." But often he taught by questions. "Whom say ye that I am?" "What think ye?" "What shall it profit a man?" "Why even of yourselves judge ye not what is right?" "What man of you?" Often he turned captious questions by asking new questions of the questioner. "Whose is the image?" "Which was neighbor?" It is as though he were asking, "What do you think?" "How do you make it out?" Apparently Jesus did not regard all human thinking as hopelessly perverted by sin.

Indeed, Jesus himself as God's Word to man is the supreme illustration of our point. The Incarnation is an evidence of God's adapting Himself to human speech. In Jesus Christ God spoke not in one dialect, but in the universal language which all men can understand, in a Man. The scriptures themselves are in the common speech of men. They used religious words, drawn often out of pagan contexts, and infused them with new content.

A really dialectical theology will take all this into account. With all that Barth says about the Word of God being God's and not man's, still it is a word directed *to* man. Otherwise, it

would not convey any message to man, who is ever a historical and culturally sensitive being. It could communicate only with a ghostly and empty form of man, the content of whose being would have to be self-engendered.[5]

Man's need is evident and it predisposes him to seek an answer. God's answer surprises him. He hoped for an answer that would leave him in self-respect, preserve his self-confidence, his independent security. But when man receives that word by faith, when he encounters God in His mercy, he understands for the first time who God is and who he himself is. God's Word at once denies man's proud questions and fulfills them by an answer man did not expect. This is the inner meaning of the dilemma with which we began. It is the dilemma that arises from man's sin and ignorance and God's righteousness and wisdom. It is here, in a true dialectic, that the answer to our question is to be found.

When the Bible and the Reformers speak of our faith being the work of the Holy Spirit, they must not be understood as saying that the Holy Spirit treats man on a less than personal level. There is mystery in the work of the Holy Spirit. We know not how the Spirit works; we see only the results. But if we use material or mechanical figures, such as "infuse," or "produce," or any term which implies that the Spirit works on the human being without his consent, then it is no longer I who believe and have faith. It is the Holy Spirit that believes in me. We have then profaned the mystery by making it magical. The product of the Holy Spirit's work is a new man, with a new center, a new knowledge of God, a new knowledge of himself. Yet he is not altogether new. For the Spirit has spoken to his "vital anguish." It has answered his questions. It has not for a moment suppressed his rational faculties.

To make our point unmistakably clear, let us suppose an experimental psychologist to be soundly converted to the Christian faith. Let us suppose him to have been a man of better than average moral character, a man brought up in a nominally Christian home, who was alienated from the church by dogmatic preaching and by the growing conviction that the human being is to be explained in terms of response to stimuli and of "built-in" patterns of behavior. He has a wife and children, for whom he has real love. He is reasonably unselfish toward his colleagues in the university, and supports progressive causes. But for him God is simply the projection of man's needs. It is obvious that as long as he holds such a conviction about himself and his world he will have no saving encounter with God. The whole notion of sin in the biblical sense is foreign to him.

Now what can happen to bring such a man to faith? Let us suppose that he did not begin by revising his scientific theory. Let us rather suppose some bitter disaster coming to him, perhaps the death of his most promising and attractive child. Whatever it is, something has upset and bewildered him, made him profoundly dissatisfied with his life and himself. Misgivings about his psychological theory beset him. Surely there must be other dimensions in human life! He is turned to the study of the New Testament and to prayer. At last faith comes to him in fulness and he finds the peace of conscience, the new joy and love, that are the fruits of faith. He is a new man. He sees himself as a sinner for the first time. His wife, his remaining children, his friends, his world take on a new meaning for him. He does not boast of his own goodness, or take pride in the cleverness of his thought that has brought him to God.

But is he completely new? The peculiarities of his mind are still the same. Laws of mathematics and laws of logic are still binding upon him. Moreover, when he goes back to his laboratory, his experimental methods are there waiting for him. What has changed? His world does look new to him. God is the most precious and joyous reality to him. Now if that faith is to hold him he must rethink the bearing of his psychological theory upon his faith. He may not change one detail of his scientific method. If he was conducting an experiment involving the escape of white rats from a maze, he may continue with it. But in his view of mankind he now understands that something more is at work than such learning as his rats undergo in repeated attempts to escape from their maze. If he tends to isolate his faith in a private sanctum, where it does not touch his daily affairs, he will inevitably lose conviction and so faith itself. But the work of reconciling his new-found faith with his problem in experimental psychology is the task of philosophy. In this work he had better keep his reason clear. For Barth to tell him that philosophy has nothing to do with his faith is a cruel closing of the doors of the Kingdom to this psychologist, *and to multitudes of others like him.* To the great discredit of the churches, this is a very common kind of cruelty.

This cruelty may spring from a variety of causes. At best it is ignorance. Yet even this ignorance is without excuse in the light of the present need of the world. It may be indolence and indifference, unwillingness to spend the labor required to share the burden of just this experimental psychologist. At worst it is fear, fear that our faith would falter and fail if we so much as touched this "worldly" problem. In that case our own faith has already lost its conviction. It would be interesting to know, and we cannot, how much of the church's unwillingness to face the crucial problems of modern philosophy is due to fear rather than to a sturdy faith. If this experimental psychologist should later renounce his faith, it would be easy for us to dismiss him by saying that his defection was due to the "offense" of the Gospel. Undeniable offense there is in the Gospel—to all our pride, our self-sufficiency, and our self-righteousness. That is offense enough!

We need to be sure that to it, or in the place of it, is not added the offense of our own false presentation of the Gospel, or that of our own spiritual pride.

However great the change that is wrought in the man of faith, he is renewed and not destroyed. There is an unbreakable continuity between his old sense of need, his frustration, his self-contradiction, that was his before faith came to him, and the new man of peace, of assurance, and of the united heart. If there is to be preaching of the Gospel, there must be a word of God addressed to the needs of men and in a language that they understand. This is the beginning of the "dialectic" between God and man. And if that word is to have meaning it must relate itself to his experience of guilt, of frustration, of fear, of weakness. If it has meaning, the sinner is moved to "put two and two together," to relate his unhappy experience to his sin. But the relating of experience involves reason. However poor traditional philosophy may have been as a guide to Christian faith, the man of faith does not dispense with thought. There is a logic of the sinner reflecting upon his guilt, a logic of the wayward son in the far country. Perhaps it is the most severe of all logic, simply because it springs out of "vital anguish."

In the case of the experimental psychologist, we made one doubtful assumption—that he could come to a saving faith without first revising his mechanistic theory of human nature. It is not unthinkable that this should occur, though even in his anguish he could not make the first move toward faith, without putting his mechanism in abeyance. It may be that theologians are too busy with more important concerns to bother with mechanistic psychology. But in that event they should recognize what they are doing. They are resigning all hope of winning most of the adherents of that view to Christian faith. In plain truth, Christian philosophy has an enormous preliminary work to do. It must look on secular versions of our world and be able to say, "Not that." Faith throws a clear light on the problem of our culture, gives guidance to philosophy, and exposes the errors in secular thought. If faith is the basic certainty, then reason has a negative service to render to faith. It must expose the rational self-contradiction of such current tendencies as naturalism, psychologism, and optimism.

A. The Rational Service of Faith

Faith cannot be indifferent to a culture whose presuppositions are hostile. In meeting this secular culture faith must employ reason. To shout is to betray our lack of faith. To coerce or to compel is not ours if we wanted it, and should be renounced if we could have it, even in the more subtle forms of social pressure. If faith is to become articulate, if it is to seek a common ground of talk, if it tries to communicate, then its appeal must be to reason. There is no other appeal. If the secular presuppositions of our culture were confined to a few professors in their studies, even then we could not be indifferent. How much less can the Church play the ostrich when these presuppositions pervade our commercial life, pervert our art, music, and literature, shout at us from the headlines of every newspaper, invade our homes through the radio, appear in public education, are implicit in our political life, in short, are in the very air that we breathe? To renounce philosophy is indeed to abandon the world. But it is more: it means that the Christian Church must, to preserve its own life, go into strict isolation; ruthlessly purge its own membership; become dictatorial over those who remain; maintain its own schools, commerce, press and cultural life; and forbid any dealing with the outside world save the most casual and formal. Even the early Church could not do that. It preserved its own compact community, especially in times of persecution. There was a "Come out from among them and be ye separate." But the early Church was not on the defensive. It was a missionary church. By the second century, it was compelled to resort to philosophy and in plain fact by the end of the fourth century it had "out-thought" as well as "outlived" the pagan world. How much less in this day of easy communication is the course of isolation possible!

All thought is implicitly universal. If I really believe a judgment to be valid, the content must hold good for all men and under every circumstance. This is plainly true in science. It also holds in matters of faith. The certainties of knowledge and of faith alike borrow heavily on social confirmation. You cannot worship a private deity. You must seek some other to share your faith. So the presence of another mind who cannot sympathize with your belief is a shaking of faith's certainty. But far more important, to live in a culture which is founded upon a denial of the very fact of God, to do business in it, to have commerce with other people on the basis of God's non-existence, is to weaken faith, if not to destroy it. Consider some of the negations which faith must make clear through reason.

1. It must protest the current tendency, especially marked in America, to build religious certainties on the foundation of natural science. Science has its important place. But it has its limits, too. It has no explanation of the knowledge of our neighbor's mind, nor can it touch the life and death questions of faith. The eagerness with which churchmen hail the latest utterances on religion from a Whitehead, a Lloyd-Morgan, an Eddington, a Jeans, is simply pathetic, as though these eminent men of science and philosophy had brought a last-minute reprieve to faith, giving it certainty just in time to save it from death! To attempt to establish faith on the foundation of science, or the scientific method, is to limit faith to whatever that method will permit. It is a complete denial of confidence in the Word of God, who alone is the source of faith's certainties. We must look with interest on the attempts of men like Wieman, Whitehead, and Dewey, when without the aid of revelation they seek the fullest religion that is possible within the limits of science. But an intelligent faith will not be surprised when their results turn out to be meager.

2. In the same way faith has its negative criticism of naturalism as an estimate of man. Because men attach utmost importance to the scientific method, they believe only in the truth of what can be discovered by that method. It is the exclusive claim of science to truth that faith must dispute. This pretentious claim denies the very condition that makes science itself possible, the knowledge of our neighbor's mind. It denies that whole side of man's nature that enables him alike to transcend nature and to transcend himself. William James once confessed that when he was tempted to this belief, he heard "that inward monitor of which W. K. Clifford once wrote, whispering the word 'bosh!' Humbug is humbug, even though it bear the scientific name." [6] But invective is not enough. Faith has a light to throw on the human mystery. To that light the rational self-contradiction of naturalism can and should be brought.

3. We have spoken of psychologism. Perhaps nothing in modern thought is so damaging to the faith of the young as the suspicion that the Object of their religious faith is a mere "projection" of the "unconscious," that their whole religious striving is an "escape." Psychologism is the perfect expression of subjective skepticism. It has its self-contradictions, too, as well as its absurdities. Yet the final, convincing answer is the personal encounter with a real Other, who negates, who judges, and who forgives us, and who therefore cannot be the mere extension of our own desires.

4. Optimism is often a real enemy of faith. It holds out sentimental and illusory hopes which subtly flatter human pride and which seek to enlist all the energies that should be at the disposal of faith. It has often invaded the pulpit. Ministers have promised their people that a little more concentrated energy, a little more intelligence, a better organization, a rolling up of their sleeves and a blowing on their hands, and the social evils of their time, yes, the very gates of Hell could not prevail against them. Exponents of world government enlist the idealism of youth. They deftly

overlook the cultural and moral conditions which are basic to a common understanding of the ends of living, a prerequisite to government of any kind. The tardiness of western Europe in achieving even a minimum harmony of economic ends, under the most apparent threats, is evidence of the enormous difficulties in the way of world government. Faith has some understanding of human pride, and especially of the power and pretense of collective pride. Faith has here an important service to chasten optimism, and thus to save mankind from what otherwise will inevitably follow, a reaction into disillusioned pessimism.

B. The Positive Service of Reason

Faith needs the work of reason in clarifying the convictions of the Church, the household of faith. Only with a strong confidence in its Gospel can the Church minister to the needs of our tragic time. Assurance and conviction are born in the personal encounter with Jesus Christ as the Word of God. But this faith must relate itself to the world of human experience. The God who is Sovereign, Judge, and Redeemer, must be related to history, to nature, to human conduct and thought. If faith pretends to dispense with reason, then it will become an impertinence in the world of human affairs.

1. The nature of revelation must be made clear. We have come to the heart of it in the New Testament doctrine of personal encounter. Revelation is no gift to satisfy idle curiosity. God does not reveal the secrets of His being to any casual inquirer. He reveals Himself only to the man who casts himself entirely upon the mercy of God. He reveals Himself in the very act of bestowing mercy and faith upon the repentant sinner. The revelation is through the encounter. But we do not meet God in naked solitude. There are the Scriptures, the law, the prophets, the apostles, and most of all, Jesus Christ. They are the objective revelation. They are indispensable. But they are not enough. They are not our revelation until we surrender the pride of our finite perspective,

until in penitence we meet the God of mercy, and until the Holy Spirit confers upon us the faith to believe. Faith is directed not to the objective revelation as such, but to the God who has thus spoken to our need.

It is with the indispensable Scriptures that our problem arises. It concerns the union of the divine and the human in the Bible. It is analogous to the problem of the two natures in Christ, which the Church was compelled to face in the fourth century. The Church can no longer afford to postpone a similarly thorough and devoted study of this relation of the divine and the human in the Scriptures. Many have seen only the divine in the Bible. They are the exponents of inerrant inspiration. Others have seen only the human in the Bible. They regard it as merely a record of Israel and of the early Church, in which is to be found a more or less reliable account of historic experiences and the interpretation of them. Even as the early Church regarded as heresy a denial either of the full humanity or the full deity of our Lord, so the modern Church should look askance at those who deny either the divine or the human element in the Bible. To see in the Old Testament only a series of problems in literary criticism is to miss its meaning and its power. We never really read the Old Testament until we stand where the people of Israel stood, until the prophets speak to us, until the righteous God of the Old Testament confronts us and our pagan society with the fact of our injustice. But to deny the human element in the Bible is to miss its relevance to our human situation. It flies in the face of obvious fact and plainly closes the Bible to many thoughtful persons.

The cardinal fact that the biblical revelation is historical, that it has taken place in time, is linked with this human element in the Bible. Without this human element the revelation simply could not be historical. These writers were plainly children of their time, subject to its limitations, burdened with its anxieties. The affairs of the Bible are exceedingly earthly. The Bible deals with laws of sanitation, of property, of debt, the having of sons, disease, death, war, politics, economics. Its stories range from vicious cruelty to the finest heroism. It was in that commonplace humanity that God revealed Himself. But beneath this surface, there are human elements that reach far into the lives of other peoples. It seems clear that some of the early Genesis stories depend upon Babylonian sources. Did the Hebrews also get their conception of the coming judgment from the Zoroastrians whom they met just after the Babylonian captivity? How early did the Law make its appearance in Israel? What is the time of the Levitical code? These and a host of similar questions are involved in the critical study of the Bible. Its meaning will be clarified as further light shines on the human element. This is the work of scholars. They must be governed by all the hard, inescapable laws of historical study. Plainly reason is the instrument. Of these studies the common believer will have little knowledge, and for them little sympathy. Yet their results, enriching his faith, must not be withheld from him in the interest of mere tradition.

2. Faith also needs the service of reason in facing the question of Christian doctrine. Revelation as personal encounter—that does not settle the question of doctrine. It aggravates it. We have already seen that this encounter is not pure feeling, as men seem to say when they deny that conceptual thinking and faith can be combined in one act. In our encounter with God we are sinners with this particular background. And we meet him as the "God, who . . ." This is the focal point toward which all Christian doctrine must move. But how to relate God as we encounter Him in faith, to the Scriptures, to history, to nature, to eschatology, this is the concern of Christian doctrine. This work can never be finished. The churches have been prematurely concerned with "systems of doctrine" and so have failed to notice many a contrary fact. But there is a relentless logic of doctrine.

3. Faith must have the assistance of reason in clarifying the ethical question. Here again the question is made more acute by the experience of divine grace. As long as we stood on our own

righteousness, we were quite content with a code of laws. They simplified our obligations and safeguarded our self-esteem. The trouble with any code of laws is always that it misses the thing of greatest import, tends to settle for lesser matters like tithing mint, anise, and cummin. You can never get into any code the weightier matters, love for God and love for man.

When the man of faith renounces his own righteousness, he does not thereby renounce the law of God. On the contrary, he is morally sensitive and awake. Obedience to God is now his passion. Love for God and love for man are now released within him. But how shall love for neighbor govern my treatment of my neighbor? It is not enough, as Kant said, to have a good will. This is central and there can be no morality without it. Nor is it enough to love God and do as you please, as Augustine put it.

What you please to do, even with a perfect love for God, which no mortal can claim, falls into a social texture. You must know that texture. For the man of faith, as for any man, the moral quality of his deed is determined in part by the consequences of that deed. Blandly to assume that if your motive (love to God and man) is right, then you can act "on principle" without regard to consequence, is to betray yourself into a callous selfishness. A father's first duty to his children is to know them, as he must if he really loves them, then be governed by that knowledge. He must be sensitive to their needs. A love which cares not for consequences is thoroughly corrupt already. The deed which flows from such a "love" will sooner or later prove disastrous.

This reliance upon motive alone, without regard to consequences, becomes even more dangerous in a complex society. The bland notion, frequently expressed in orthodox circles, that you have only to convert men to the love of God and their social conduct will automatically correct itself, has been disastrous. It has permitted all kinds of social injustice to hide under the cloak of the most innocent-looking piety. Small wonder that the victims of those injustices have regarded religion as an opiate! The Christian has a duty to knowledge. It is a knowledge not merely of other individuals, but a duty to understand his time, the issues that are alive, the economic pressures under which he and his neighbors live, the social trends that are at work. Here again, reason makes its indispensable contribution to faith.

The man of faith needs to remember his own sin of pride. In the act of saving faith pride received its death sentence. Yet it dies a slow death. Here is one "concept" which he needs ever to keep before himself. Pride is very subtle, very persistent. The man of faith may presently find himself feeling good about his own first victories over sin, about his own faith that is growing stronger, his own superior grasp of divine realities, and end by disaster to himself and to others. The havoc wrought by self-righteous sons of grace in the world makes a long and very sorry story.

He needs to remember that pride becomes all the more demonic in social groups. When I serve my class, my nation, my race, my denomination, I have the assurance of self-effacing devotion to a cause. Under that respectable moral cloak I may then conceal my share of the demonic pride of my group, which invariably works injustice to members of other groups. This knowledge of collective pride will help us to be more effective servants of our groups. This knowledge of the corruption of power will also save us from utopian hopes; save us from spending our energies on illusory short-cuts in the saving of society; enable us to spend our limited strength where it will really count; enable us to be better citizens of our nation and of our world. One of the essential contributions of Christian faith to the contemporary social scene is its insight into the subtlety and perversity of sinful pride in places of power.

Again, the experience of grace enables you to see your fellows in their true light. What you believe men to be will govern your treatment of them. A philosophy which puts a low value on the human person will inevitably result in ethical behavior that treats

men on that low level. Believe that men are only elaborate response mechanisms, and you will tend to treat them as such. The
afterglow of Christian belief in your parents may preserve in you
some semblance of the Christian estimate of man. But your children's children will lack that advantage. Say of man that he is a
creature and servant of the state and presently tyranny and
brutality will break loose. Conduct follows belief. It is for this
reason that metaphysics is so momentous.

As a man of faith you will be governed by that faith in what
you see in your fellows. You will understand that they, like you,
are sinners. But potentially they are sons and daughters of God.
Since they have that possibility through the grace of God, you
will be ready to protest and resist any injustice, any cruelty, any
debasing attitude, that treats them as any less than possible citizens
of the Kingdom of God. Every failure of yours so to act is an
inevitable weakening of your own faith. We may gather up the
ethical duty of the man of faith into the form of a Kantian categorical imperative: So act that by your deeds, words and attitudes,
you will help to bring men into a saving faith in Jesus Christ. This
is the whole law and the prophets.

CHAPTER 9

The Case for Christianity

What kind of knowledge of God is possible? That depends upon the interests we propose to satisfy in that knowledge. Are the interests that lead us toward a knowledge of God casual? More than a casual knowledge of God will not be forced upon us. Are our interests vital? We may find the knowledge of which the New Testament speaks. If we travel the road of sincere repentance we shall have the knowledge that is made possible by faith. If our interest is mainly rational, we shall arrive at speculative uncertainty. Such knowledge as we gain will be highly abstract, like the knowledge of the demons who believe and tremble.[1] If this rational attempt could be completely successful, without the radical change of our vital interests, it would be a false knowledge, no matter how "correct" the form of words.

This conclusion, to which our argument has led us, should throw some light on the task of Christian apologetics. We have heard much recently about the need for a new apologetic. What was wrong with the old one? (1) It often surrendered the ground of Christian faith at the outset. It took its stand within the naturalistic tradition, and from these assumptions tried to prove that God was a not-yet-untenable hypothesis. Underlying the old method was the assumption that the only kind of certainty was the compulsion of mathematically exact proof. Such attempts must end in rational uncertainty. No proof has been devised that wins universal consent. All "proofs" fail accordingly to pass the crucial test of objectivity. The unbeliever is the standing rebuke to this hope for rational certainty about God. Believers have often professed to find the rational evidence quite satisfactory. But the crucial test of

147

social confirmation showed that they were borrowing upon the certainties of faith to give weight to their argument.

(2) The old apologetic sundered external from internal meaning. It assumed that rational certainty could be established apart from faith; that if this certainty were made clear, then the life of faith would follow. At least the principal barriers would be removed and the ground cleared for the vital encounter with God. This separation of faith and reason is not only undesirable: it would be like getting into Heaven by some back door. Quite distinct from the question of desirability, such knowledge is impossible. The central insights about God are revealed through the vital encounter of faith, or not at all. The old apologetic neglected the subtle perversion of thought by unworthy vital interests, the perversion that takes its clearest form for us in the exaltation of our private perspective into the norm for man and for God. God and man ought to see life through our eyes. One consequence of this oversight was the tacit assumption that God ought to answer our questions; that His rationality should approve itself to our perspective; that there was no serious defect either in the form of our questions or in the private interests that framed the questions.

We have said that the case for Christianity stands or falls with the biblical diagnosis of the human predicament. This universal malady of man is most evident in person to person encounters, where vital interests are at stake. It was much easier to believe in original sin in an agrarian economy, where a man's interests were vividly clear to his neighbors. Small, compact communities do not foster comforting illusions about human perfectibility. Even in a good home the failure to be responsible is clear for all to see.

But our modern culture has dehumanized and depersonalized man. Our complex economic structure facilitates the pretenses of the individual. It hides from a man's eyes both the vast complex of human service which is the source of his good, and the damaging results of his proud pretensions which are indistinguishably merged with the collective mass of human evil. Most of his contacts are casual and mediated by the intricate machinery of modern life. He does not see himself nor his fellows as persons. The social studies have furthered this basic confusion. Psychology has tended increasingly to treat the human being as an object of study, obscuring his being as a subject. A few extreme writers have even denied the existence of the subject altogether, blandly unaware that they themselves must assume some kind of subject before their propositions can have logical meaning. The other social sciences have treated not the individual, but the group, as the only source of any verifiable information. Modern society gives the worker a social security number and the soldier a number on his identification tags. In this depersonalized life, where the roots of the common life in the individual are obscured, it is small wonder that the notion of original sin has lost its persuasiveness.

It is interesting to see in French existentialism a violent revolt against the depersonalizing of man and an equally violent assertion of the existence of the self in its own right. Insofar as existentialism is a recoil from the abstractions of the social studies to the concreteness of human freedom, it is healthy and long overdue. Yet this movement, for the most part not chastened by the recognition of human pride and arrogance, goes to the opposite extreme of self-deification. The human self is made into an absolute, given a weight of importance that it cannot possibly bear. So far the existentialists have been at a loss to construct any but the vaguest social philosophy. Sartre claims to be a revolutionary. But his program is largely negative. Existentialism is chiefly important as a symptom of violent protest over the dehumanizing of man.

But the fact of original sin, obscured as it is in the baffling complexities of modern society, is still a fact. Sensitive eyes can see it at work. We see evidences of it in other individuals and their injustice, for example in the motorist who "takes his half out of the middle of the road." We still have to do with individuals enough to recognize in others the *hybris* which is the most obvious manifestation of original sin. The ability to recognize this same *hybris* in ourselves is another matter. The grace to turn that judgment, by which we see the self-interest of others, upon ourselves is one of the first fruits of faith.

But the proud pretension of finite perspective, which is the intellectual fruitage of original sin, becomes demonic when it operates in powerful social groups. Nations engaged in wars, where their very existence is at stake, always assume the moral rightness of their cause. Information that would cast serious doubt upon the justice of a nation is deliberately suppressed, usually with the consent of the citizens. Not until later years are the damaging facts allowed to be made public.

Any man can recognize original sin where power is concentrated. History is replete with illustrations of the corruption which power works on its holders. Athens turned the Confederation of Delos into an empire to serve its own interests and brought the flowering of her culture to a premature end.[2] Rome at the height of its power was so dazzled by its own splendor that it could not see the obvious decay within its own life that would bring it to ruin. The medieval Church came to power in the wake of Hildebrand's reforms. The corruption of the Holy See, which culminated in the late fifteenth century, is a sad and familiar story. The Counter-Reformation was not possible until the Church had lost most of its temporal power. More recently governments have gained new power over their citizens through the skills placed in their hands by the social studies. The holders of power have learned how to use the idealism of their people to fortify their own position, which permits them cynically to pervert the loyalty of the people to their own private advantage. Communism, which professes to serve the masses over the world, becomes an instrument of Russian policy. Instances could be multiplied.

In our own country it is a commonplace that democracy can survive only when power is kept decentralized. This fear of power concentration informed the writers of the Constitution. Prolonged periods of power for any one party have always been attended by corruption, locally as well as nationally. This is the common defense of our two-party system. The slogan, "Turn the rascals out," is eloquent. "His Majesty's Loyal Opposition" reveals British political acumen.

It is also a commonplace that when power is threatened, the holders of power usually redouble their oppression, making only such concessions as are necessary to preserve their place of power. This holds true of both management and labor. An ethically informed mind should expect no more moral excellence from one group than from the other. The principle holds in the conduct of racial majorities. When the racial issue is sharp, the dominant majority always reveals its arrogance in such phrases as "Let them know their place," with the implication that "their" rights have less standing than those of the majority.

The principle holds among religious groups. When the churches have come into places of political power, they also have been corrupted. Apologists for the Roman Church openly avow the policy of claiming toleration when they are in the minority, and disowning this same policy when they are in the majority, on the ground that "error has not the same rights as the truth." [3] The struggle of Protestant minorities for toleration, which they in turn denied to other sects when they came to power, tells the same story. Competing denominations in local communities and rival groups competing for power in individual congregations, illustrate the moral blindness which afflicts groups in power. Power corrupts the moral judgment of men.

We propose, then, that the new apologetic start from this obvious and ominous fact. Let the fact be frankly faced. Let its meaning be analyzed and its implications made clear. This analysis will throw a clear light on the difficulty that inheres in the social studies. Objectivity can be achieved only in the moral harmony of rival special interests. Until this fact is clearly accepted, men argue with one another over vital interests. Literally their minds cannot meet because they are not talking the same language. The semantic difficulty can be met only on the moral level.

To begin with the fact of the perversion of finite perspective, with "original sin," will give to the new apologetic some distinct advantages over the old. (1) It has a solid factual basis, the perversion of self-interest in both the individual and society. (2) It faces from the outset the intimate relation between internal and external meaning. It recognizes the subjective meaning of experience. (3) It will point toward a living rather than an abstract solution of man's predicament. To state the problem in this form is to open the way toward a saving encounter with the mercy of God. It does not end in an abstract concept. This may sound like prejudging the outcome of the argument from the beginning. But Christian apologetic has every right to put its case in this way; to show that its analysis of human nature and human trouble makes sense; and that the solution offered in the Gospel is the only salvation commensurate with human need. This is precisely what competing philosophies do. Disinterestedness in philosophy is a pretense.

We can best illustrate the new apologetic if we can agree on the most urgent contemporary concern. Where is the decisive issue of our day? What is that focal point to which Christian faith must direct its message and thereby touch every living human interest? Surely it is the problem of individuality in community. Whitehead calls this "the topic of religion." [4] Individuality and community stand today in open conflict. If faith has some word that will clarify the conflict, reveal the dimensions of the issues, point the way to an answer, it will at the same time find its most direct word on behalf of the Gospel, and will release the power of the Gospel at the very center of man's weakness and despair.

This conflict takes the current form of a struggle between the individual and the state. In the present confusion, the individualist often appeals to the state to defend his rights, then rebels against the restrictions of the state that are invoked in the name of other peoples' rights. At least in America, there are few pure collectivists or individualists. The conflict between the individual and the state is thus in part a conflict within the individual himself. The claimant individualist becomes an ardent collectivist when the interests under discussion are changed.

The individualist makes false claims for himself. He fondly imagines that the state is by nature and of right a collection of individuals. Occasionally such a theory still appears in print. But in fact individualism is not primitive. Primitive man existed only as a member of a tribe and was both physically and psychologically dependent upon the tribe. To be exiled from his tribe was a fate worse than death. The sense of being completely lost was far more intense for the exiled savage than it is for the homesick freshman, away from home for the first time. Historically, individualism is a kind of luxury which some societies cannot afford. Where it does develop, the conditions that make it possible are clearly a social product.

But the individualist finds it convenient to forget all this history. He forgets also his enormous debt to the society which has nurtured him. He exaggerates the importance of his own contributions to the social good. By this perversion of his judgment he is led to claims that far exceed the bounds of justice. If he belongs to a class whose privileges are fortified by existing laws, he receives more than he gives, not only economically, but culturally, morally, politically as well. It is impossible to exaggerate this social malady of irresponsibility. It is illustrated by the widespread clamor of people for their rights in contrast with the very mild murmur about duties. But society cannot extend any right to me, unless someone, somewhere takes on an added load of duty. Rights that are conferred are drafts against the moral capital of a society, a capital that can be replenished only by the responsible performance of duty. Any society, therefore, that has more rights than duties is already in moral bankruptcy, however long the appearance of its economic soundness may be preserved. Royce once went so far as to say, "I

have only one inalienable right—the opportunity to do my duty." [5]
We can illustrate the serious nature of this moral disease of irresponsibility by reminding ourselves that if everyone were paid
the wages or salary that he thought he deserved, any economy
would go bankrupt. With this analysis most would be inclined to
agree, provided it did not apply to themselves. This is where the
malady comes home.

The very complexity of modern social life helps to preserve this
pretense. Whatever money a man possesses, however he may
have come by it, fosters the illusion of his own power and self-
sufficiency. Can he not go out and buy what he needs, if prices
are not unreasonable? As for his failures, he has become expert
in tracing their causal antecedents, away from his own front door!
In a more primitive community it was harder to evade responsibility. A man's neighbors could trace his failure to his own im-
providence. But in a complex society, where a man's life is the
meeting place of forces that come from the ends of the earth, it is
easy to blame someone else, no matter what goes wrong. So he
blames his parents, his early training, his defective education, his
teachers, his employees, his union heads, the New Deal, the welfare state, the communists, the profiteers, the fascists, his wife, his
neighbors, his church. The sin of the individual in community is
irresponsibility.

On the other hand, the collectivist always obscures the debts of
society to the individual. The very complexity of modern life
emphasizes man's interdependence. His economic life is plainly
intertwined with that of all of his fellow-citizens. Today a man's
economic health is bound up with the welfare of people on the
other side of the globe. Not many decades ago, the status of the
public schools in Mississippi was the exclusive concern of the citizens of that state. But today its children grow up and move to every
other state in the nation, thus creating a nation-wide interest in
the state of public education in Mississippi. Well within living
memory, the condition of the road between Richmond and Wil-

liamsburg was the concern only of the farmers who lived along that road, together with the few citizens of Richmond and Williamsburg who had occasion to travel it. Now the condition of that road is the concern, and may become the cause of complaint, of motorists from the entire continent.

But in making these and similar claims on behalf of the community, the exponents of the common life overlook an enormous debt which society owes to individuals. Without the individual no scientific, political, artistic, moral, or religious progress is possible. The long line of wise men, experimenters, prophets, political innovators have been the chief benefactors of their society. But they purchased the right to be benefactors by a brave kind of rebellion against the common ways of their group. Individualism is a luxury only to primitive societies and those which are threatened with destruction. For any growing society, individualism is no longer a luxury, but a necessity. Dull conformity is the death of culture, of religion, of science, of art, as well as of democracy.

Yet mankind has unbounded confidence in the validity of human groups as an adequate center of his loyalty. The good society is still within his grasp. This hope manifests itself in humanism as a religion. The philosophical background of humanism, which makes the good society at once the origin and the goal of religious life, is found in the thought of Emile Durkheim, French anthropologist. Durkheim based his conclusions on the study of totemism as a form of social organization among primitive tribes. He concluded that religion is purely social; that its mythology is a disguise which permits society subconsciously to exercise its power and authority over the individual, using the gods, their traditions and their ritual, to give dignity and majesty to the claims of the group. Society itself is the real source of religious authority, the really majestic being. Religious experience consists in the exhilaration of belonging to the group. Conscience is the disguised voice of social pressure within the life of the individual. Modern religious humanism is the direct descendant of this view, holding that man is the object of true reverence, man in his ideal social state. The whole duty of man is to subordinate himself to the good society.

This appears to be the most direct and wholly simple way of solving what we have called the crucial problem of our day. But it contains three fatal defects.

1. The practical difficulty which such a theory creates has been amply illustrated in recent times. If morals are purely relative to the group, then the group itself is above right and wrong. The individual then has no rational defense against the tyranny of the group. His only alternative lies between an acquiescence in which his own moral judgment is suffocated, or a rebellion in which he is under the spell of his own self-aggrandizement. Every society is itself under a moral judgment. This was one of the profound insights of the Old Testament prophets, who brought God's judgment upon Israel and upon Judah for their injustice and idolatry. They conceived the enemies of Israel as the instruments of God's wrath upon Israel, the enemies themselves also being under the judgment of God. It was this conviction which enabled the prophets, not to echo the moral opinions of the crowd, but to turn against their own society, to condemn its old ways, and either to enunciate a new moral demand or to recover and clarify an old one, all in the name of God. Whenever any society has denied its own fallibility and its own subordination to the judgment of God, it thus tampers with its own conscience. So whenever the demi-gods of state have usurped the place of God, this prophetic dissenter is the first target of their violence, as witness the late Nazi dictatorship and the present regime in Russia. They can tolerate no deviations, no allegiance to a God above the state, in whose name the exclusive claims of the state would be in constant jeopardy. When society throws off the "disguise" of religion, which it must inevitably do if it recognizes Durkheim's claims as true, then it must become tyrannical over the individual. By the same sign, the one dependable bulwark against the tyranny of the state is found in believers

in the God "who alone is Lord of the conscience," and who must therefore bring their own actions as citizens, together with the demands which the state makes upon them, before the judgment of God. A purely humanistic state will find itself without those resources of conscience which make democracy even remotely possible and will therefore inevitably become a tyranny. If the vice of the individual in community is irresponsibility, the vice of the community is tyranny.

2. No society can ever make the individual completely real to itself. Even the good home, where individuals are best known, never completely knows its members. But to be completely known is one of the deepest needs of men. The praise of our friends in their generous moods never takes into full account the evil that is in us. Human blame never approximates full justice and is usually vitiated by a self-righteousness that feeds itself by finding evil in others. The world's rough judgment sees only the outward deed, never the important inner meaning. It takes only such part of a man's work as has economic value, or pleases some vagrant fancy, pays him what it must, and ignores what is unique and most important, the very condition that makes his best work possible.

> Not on the vulgar mass
> Called "work," must sentence pass,
> Things done, that took the eye and had the price;
> O'er which, from level stand,
> The low world laid its hand,
> Found straightway to its mind, could value in a trice:
>
> But all, the world's coarse thumb
> And finger failed to plumb,
> So passed in making up the main account;
> All instincts immature,
> All purposes unsure,
> That weighed not as his work, yet swelled the man's amount:
>
> Thoughts hardly to be packed
> Into a narrow act,

Fancies that broke through language and escaped;
All I could never be,
All, men ignored in me,
This, I was worth to God. . . .[6]

3. The community demands responsibility from its members,
yet it is powerless to create it. It can foster it by national observ-
ances, patriotic songs, public rallies, pageants, and by rewards and
punishments. Every social institution prizes its sentiments that en-
courage loyalty. Often this sentiment of loyalty is fostered at the
expense of some "foreign" group. Leaders fortify their power by
deliberately cultivating this implicit hostility, playing upon the
fears of their own members, seeking thus to solidify their own
place. Recent history has furnished many illustrations of this
cruelty: "Aryan" against Jew, communist against fascist, capi-
talist against worker, white against Negro, American against "de-
signing Europeans," Protestant against Catholic.

Public opinion is, of course, the most potent agent for mobilizing
responsibility. It would be interesting to know, and we cannot,
how large a part of the world's best work is done because of the
hope of praise, or the fear of censure. Yet even the most compact
public opinion cannot create responsibility within the individual.
Work that is done "to be seen of men" is always aware of its own
appearance of virtue, never succeeds in becoming genuine, honest, "from the heart." The community cannot survive without individual responsibility, yet that source of its life lies beyond its
power. John Dewey wrote in 1938 that the principal change in his
belief in the preceding eight years was in his growing awareness of
the importance of the individual.

I should now wish to emphasize more than I formerly did that individuals are the finally decisive factors of the nature and movement of
associated life. . . . I am led to emphasize the idea that only the
voluntary coöperation of individuals can produce social institutions
that will protect the liberties necessary for achieving development of
genuine individuality.[7]

The very survival of a society thus depends upon a moral capital which itself cannot create. The attempt of any society to be absolute is clearly suicidal. The nation (or class) that deifies itself is by the same act dooming itself to destruction. Like any human institution, it is under moral judgment. This fact of being under moral judgment is an indispensable condition of genuine freedom. A good society must respect the unseen sources of responsibility in its members, see that their conscience is kept free. Without the free exercise of personal responsibility, the spiritual resources of a nation dry up.

The clear choice which modern man faces, therefore, is not between pretentious individualism and the tyrannical state. Pure individualism is never possible, least of all in a highly complex society where men are bound in a common life by multiple rights and duties. The choice is rather between the statism which makes an absolute out of the nation, suppresses the freedom and spontaneity of the individual on the one hand, and on the other the socially responsible freedom of men, whose self-centered idolatry has been chastened by an encounter with the grace of God. It is the choice between tyrannical control and voluntary control. Yet the choice is not a simple one. We must at once modify these alternatives. For the possibility that the perversion of judgment and conduct by self-interest can ever be overcome in history is very remote. Even in the devoutly penitent life the sin of pride is still at work. To expect that human freedom will ever become socially responsible on a scale large enough to dispense with laws is utopian indeed. Even the most ardent exponents of price-mechanism economics recognize the need of large-scale regulations to safeguard the public against monopoly, to protect and compensate innocent victims of sudden economic change, to establish controls against those who would exploit ignorance, and to see that as far as possible equality of opportunity is granted to all. But no one is wise enough to say how far the inner controls of faith may go toward reducing the necessity of outward constraint. The possibilities in that direction are without any known limits.

Christian political action will keep these things in mind. It will protest the concentration of power in the hands of any political party or of owners of industry or of any small group of men, no matter how idealistic their pretensions. It will recognize the need of increasing controls as the economic and social interdependencies of mankind become more complex, and will favor such controls as will make for greater justice, without drying up the roots of society in the creative freedom of the individual. Most of all, it will seek to increase the number of those whose pretentious claims upon society have been humbled by exposure to the grace of God. Without that faithful work of the Church, statism is assured of a speedy triumph, bringing disaster upon the spirit of man. Individuality is possible only among responsible citizens who know well that if one member of the body suffers, all the members suffer with it.

This crucial conflict between individuality and community is really an appeal to the mercy of God. Let the Church say so! Her apologetic will thus be *en rapport* with the basic needs of her day and will be a fulfillment of her own prophetic tradition.

We have spoken of responsibility as the alternative to tyranny. How can responsibility be attained? Only by a word so powerful, so clear, so persuasive, that a man's pretentious claims will be exposed to himself. Only one answer has ever really been made to this, the crucial question of human life. It is the Christian answer. Christian faith confronts a man with a fair judgment of himself. He can never judge himself; no society can ever be just to him. Exposed to the judgment of God, he must renounce all evasion, cease blaming others for his failures, identify himself with his past sins and confess, "I have sinned."

But how can men be brought to that humility before God? The appeal must be directed in part to the integrity of man. Broken as this integrity is by sin, it is not destroyed. Man has some capacity to recognize that all is not well with himself. His resources are not enough. His self-sufficiency fails him under stress. No Christian faith is possible until a man has integrity enough to confront his own sin, to face his own evasions, and to accept his responsibility to God.

The Gospel has an ally in man's own restless spirit. He is often lonely, afraid, helpless, lost. He can understand what Jeremiah meant when he said of his people that they had "hewed them out cisterns, broken cisterns, that can hold no water." [8] He can understand, too, the word of the young man in the far country, "I perish here with hunger." [9]

Pretense is a heavy load to carry. To maintain his pretense of decency a man must always be on guard. He must suppress ugly memories. He must avoid people whose superiority might damage his self-esteem. He must contrive not to meet up with Jesus Christ. But to be constantly on guard wearies him. Dishonesty consumes his energies. He gets weary and heavy-laden in spite of himself. He lives in fear, not so much that God may judge him, or that others may discover him, as that he should find out—himself. His pretense of decency shuts him out from deep friendship.

There appears to be a conscience in mankind which severely punishes the man who does not somehow and at some time, at whatever cost to his pride, cease to defend and assert himself, and instead confess himself fallible and human. Until he can do this, an impenetrable wall shuts him out from the living experience of feeling himself a man among men.[10]

In the encounter with Jesus Christ, his pretense is exposed for the shabby thing that it is. His own darkness is brought to the Light. When a man really confronts himself in the presence of God, he can only cry out for the mercy of God. In that moment he has no other recourse. He now knows that without the forgiveness of God, he can have no peace of conscience. Here the fears that dissuaded him from honesty are quieted. Here he sees himself as he really is. He is "objective" for the first time. He no longer need defend himself. God has searched him out, exposed him, and forgiven him. God is now God once more, his hope, his defense, his high tower. He is restored to his lost humanity. While the battle against his pride will continue throughout life, it will henceforth be a winning rather than a losing struggle, if he keeps faith. This is what it means to know God. The Christian knowledge of God is an existential knowledge. It involves the whole man. To come to a knowledge of God and of ourselves is, as John Calvin once said, "true and substantial wisdom." [11]

Selected Bibliography

CHAPTER I

Bennett, Charles A., *The Dilemma of Religious Knowledge* (New Haven: Yale University Press, 1931).

Blanshard, Brand, *The Nature of Thought* (London: George Allen & Unwin Ltd., 1939), chapters 2–6.

Hocking, William Ernest, *The Meaning of God in Human Experience* (New Haven: Yale University Press, 1928), chapters 4, 5.

Kroner, Richard, *The Primacy of Faith* (New York: The Macmillan Co., 1943).

Unamuno, Miguel De, *The Tragic Sense of Life*, tr. J. E. Crawford Flitch (London: Macmillan & Co., 1921), chapters 1, 2, 5, and 6.

Werkmeister, W. H., *The Basis and Structure of Knowledge* (New York: Harper & Brothers, 1948), chapters 3, 4.

CHAPTER 2

Blanshard, *op. cit.*, chapter 14.

Hocking, *op. cit.*, chapters 10–12.

Niebuhr, H. Richard, *The Meaning of Revelation* (New York: The Macmillan Co., 1941), chapter 1.

Niebuhr, Reinhold, *The Nature and Destiny of Man* (New York: Charles Scribner's Sons, 1941), Vol. I, chapter 2.

Royce, Josiah, *The Religious Aspect of Philosophy* (Boston: Houghton, Mifflin & Co., 1885), chapter 9.

Royce, Josiah, *The World and the Individual* (New York: The Macmillan Co., 1923), Vol. I, lecture 7.

CHAPTER 3

St. Anselm, translations of *Proslogium* and *Monologium* by Sidney Norton Deane (Chicago: Open Court Publishing Co., 1910).

Farmer, Herbert H., *Towards Belief in God* (New York: The Macmillan Co., 1943), chapters 3, 11.

Hocking, *op. cit.*, chapter 22.

Kant, Immanuel, *The Critique of Pure Reason* (New York: The Macmillan Co., 1936), marginal pp. 567–642, 738–831.

Sorley, W. R., *Moral Values and the Idea of God* (Cambridge: The University Press, 1919), chapters 12, 13, 16–19.

Tennant, F. R., *Philosophical Theology* (Cambridge: The University Press, 1937), Vol. II, chapter 4.

CHAPTER 4

Bixler, J. S., *et. al.*, *The Nature of Religious Experience* (New York: Harper & Brothers, 1937).

Dewey, John, *A Common Faith* (New Haven: Yale University Press, 1934).

Feuerbach, Ludwig, *The Essence of Christianity*, tr. Marian Evans (London: John Chapman, 1854).

James, William, *The Varieties of Religious Experience* (New York: Longmans, Green & Co., 1902), lectures 19, 20.

Macintosh, D. C., *Theology as an Empirical Science* (New York: The Macmillan Co., 1919).

Macintosh, D. C., *The Problem of Religious Knowledge* (New York: Harper & Brothers, 1940).

Trueblood, D. Elton, *The Knowledge of God* (New York: Harper & Brothers, 1939).

Wieman, Henry Nelson, *Religious Experience and the Scientific Method* (New York: The Macmillan Co., 1926).

Wieman, Henry Nelson, *The Source of Human Good* (Chicago: The University of Chicago Press, 1946).

Wieman, H. N. and Meland, B. E., *American Philosophies of Religion* (New York: Harper & Brothers, 1936).

CHAPTER 5

Baillie, John, *Our Knowledge of God* (New York: Charles Scribner's Sons, 1939), pp. 107–118.

Barth, Karl, *Dogmatics in Outline*, tr. G. T. Thomson (New York: Philosophical Library, 1949), chapters 1–5.

Natural Theology, translations of Karl Barth, *Nein!* and Emil Brunner,

Natur und Gnade by Peter Fraenkel (London: Geoffrey Bles: The Centenary Press, 1946).

Brother Benignus (Gerrity), *Nature, Knowledge and God* (Milwaukee: The Bruce Publishing Co., 1947), chapters 20, 21.

Farrell, Walter, *A Companion to the Summa*, Vol. I (New York: Sheed and Ward, 1941), chapter 2.

Gilson, Etienne, *Christianity and Philosophy*, tr. Ralph Macdonald (New York: Sheed and Ward, 1939).

Gilson, Etienne, *The Philosophy of St. Thomas Aquinas*, tr. Edward Bullough (St. Louis: B. Herder Book Co., 2nd ed., 1929), chapters 3, 4, 5.

Phillips, R. P., *Modern Thomistic Philosophy* (London: Burns, Oates and Washbourne, Ltd., 1935; Westminster, Md.: Newman Press, 1946), Vol. II, pp. 261–302.

Thomas Aquinas, *Summa Contra Gentiles*, tr. by Dominican Fathers (London: Burns, Oates and Washbourne, Ltd., 1924), Vol. I, chapters 4–14.

Thomas Aquinas, *Summa Theologica*, tr. by Dominican Fathers (London: Burns, Oates and Washbourne, Ltd., 1911; New York: Benziger Brothers, Inc.), Vol. I, Questions 2–12.

Casserley, J. V. Langmead, *The Christian in Philosophy* (London: Faber and Faber, 1949), chapter 2.

CHAPTER 6

Bowman, A. A., *Studies in the Philosophy of Religion* (London: Macmillan & Co., 1938), Vol. II, chapters 23–26.

Buber, Martin, *Between Man and Man*, tr. Ronald Gregor Smith (New York: The Macmillan Co., 1948), chapters 1, 2.

Hocking, *op. cit.*, chapters 17–19.

Niebuhr, Reinhold, *op. cit.*, Vol. II, chapter 8.

Royce, *The Religious Aspect of Philosophy* (Boston: Houghton Mifflin Company, 1885), pp. 149–162.

CHAPTERS 7 AND 8

Aulen, Gustav, *The Faith of the Christian Church*, tr. Eric H. Wahlstrom and G. Everett Arden (Philadelphia: The Muhlenberg Press, 1948), Part I.

Baillie, *op. cit.*, pp. 119–143.

Brunner, Emil, *Revelation and Reason,* tr. Olive Wyon (Philadelphia: The Westminster Press, 1946), chapters 1–13.

Hazelton, Roger, *Renewing the Mind* (New York: The Macmillan Co., 1949), chapters 1, 4, 6, 7.

Niebuhr, Reinhold, *op. cit.,* Vol. I, chapters 7–9, Vol. II, chapters 4, 5.

Richardson, Alan, *Christian Apologetics* (New York: Harper & Brothers, 1947), chapters 6, 9–10.

CHAPTER 9

Brunner, Emil, *Man in Revolt,* tr. Olive Wyon (New York: Charles Scribner's Sons, 1939), chapter 12.

Haroutunian, Joseph, *Lust for Power* (New York: Charles Scribner's Sons, 1949).

Inter-Seminary Series (New York: Harper & Brothers, 1946), Book 1.

Niebuhr, Reinhold, *op. cit.,* Vol. II, chapter 9.

Tillich, Paul, *The Religious Situation,* tr. H. Richard Niebuhr (New York: Henry Holt and Co., 1932).

Notes

Unless otherwise noted, Old Testament quotations are from the American Standard Version, New Testament quotations from the Revised Standard Version.

2. *Isaiah* 40:25.
3. *Romans* 11:33.
4. *Exodus* 3:13.
5. *Exodus* 4:1.
6. *Exodus* 5:2.
7. Immanuel Kant, *The Critique of Pure Reason*, tr. F. Max Müller (New York: The Macmillan Co., 1922), p. 700.
8. William Ernest Hocking, *The Meaning of God in Human Experience* (New Haven: Yale University Press, 1928), p. 225.
9. *The Dilemma of Religious Knowledge* (New Haven: Yale University Press, 1931), p. 19.
10. *The Knowledge of God*, tr. J. L. M. Haire and Ian Henderson (New York: Charles Scribner's Sons, 1939), p. 6.
11. *Ibid.*, p. 9.
12. *The Philosophy of Religion*, tr. A. J. D. Farrer and Bertram Lee Woolf (London: Ivor Nicholson and Watson Ltd., 1937), pp. 56, 55.
13. Hocking, *op. cit.*, p. xiii.
14. Aldous Huxley, *Antic Hay* (New York: Harper & Brothers), p. 8.
15. Miguel De Unamuno, *The Tragic Sense of Life*, tr. J. E. Crawford Flitch (London: Macmillan & Co., 1921), pp. 168, 169, 184.
16. *Isaiah* 55:9.
17. Alfred Lord Tennyson, "In Memoriam," LIV.
18. *The Primacy of Faith* (New York: The Macmillan Co., 1943), pp. 94, 147.
19. *Op. cit.*, p. 55.
20. See W. H. Werkmeister, *The Basis and Structure of Knowledge* (New York: Harper & Brothers, 1948), chapters 3 and 4. See also

Brand Blanshard, *The Nature of Thought* (London: George Allen & Unwin Ltd., 1939), chapters 4–6.

21. St. Augustine, *De Libero Arbitrio*, tr. Francis E. Tourscher (Philadelphia: The Peter Reilly Company, 1937), Book 2, chapt. 8, pp. 147–149.

22. Reinhold Niebuhr, *The Nature and Destiny of Man* (New York: Charles Scribner's Sons, 1941), Vol. I, pp. 195–196.

23. *Luke* 9:49.   24. Niebuhr, *op. cit.*, p. 195.

25. David Hume: *A Treatise of Human Nature* (London: J. M. Dent & Sons Ltd., 1920; Section 6, Everyman's Library, New York: E. P. Dutton & Co., Inc., 1920), Vol. I, p. 239.

CHAPTER 2

1. But see H. Richard Niebuhr's luminous insight on the relative position occupied by every student of history in his *The Meaning of Revelation*, chapter 1. (New York: The Macmillan Co., 1941).

2. Josiah Royce, *Fugitive Essays* (Cambridge: Harvard University Press, 1925), p. 347.

3. Royce, *The World and the Individual* (New York: The Macmillan Company, 1899), Vol. I, p. 374.

4. *Ibid.*, Vol. II, pp. 29–30.

5. William Shakespeare, *Hamlet*, Act III, sc. 3.

6. *The Practical Significance of Pessimism*, written 1879, p. 30.

7. William James, *The Will to Believe* (New York: Longmans, Green, & Co., 1919), p. 21.

8. This does not mean that social consensus establishes the reality of an object, but that the objective is public rather than private in character.

9. Royce, *op. cit.*, pp. 291–292. The reference in Aristotle is to *Physics*, Bk. I, Sect. 1.

10. *Isaiah* 40:25.

11. *Op. cit.*, p. 458.

12. *The Principles of Logic* (London: William Clowes and Sons Ltd., 1883), Chapter II, paragraphs 7, 8.

13. Royce, *The Conception of God* (New York: The Macmillan Co., 1897), p. 262.

14. Royce, *The Philosophy of Loyalty* (New York: The Macmillan Co., 1908), p. 172.

15. Kroner, *op. cit.*, p. 94.   16. Tennyson, *op. cit.*, XLII.

CHAPTER 3

1. *St. Anselm*, tr. Sidney Norton Deane (Chicago: Open Court Publishing Co., 1910), pp. 10, 19.
2. Fragments 4, 5, quoted in John Burnet, *Early Greek Philosophy*, fourth edition (London: Adam and Charles Black, 1930), p. 173.
3. *Op. cit.*, p. 312.   4. *Op. cit.*, p. 151.
5. *Ibid.*, p. 158.
6. *Meditations*, V, in *Selections*, ed. Ralph M. Eaton (New York: Charles Scribner's Sons, 1927), p. 140.
7. Kant, *op. cit.*, pp. 479–480 (marginal pp. 594–595).
8. *Ibid.*, p. 479 (marg. p. 593).
9. *Appearance and Reality* (London: Swan Sonnenschein & Co., 1893), p. 396.
10. T. E. Jessup in *The Christian Understanding of Man*, Oxford Conference Series (London: George Allen & Unwin Ltd., 1938), p. 37.
11. *Op. cit.*, p. 315.   12. *Ibid.*, p. xvi.
13. "*What* things are, extended, moving, colored, tuneful, majestic, beautiful, holy, *what* they are in any aspect of their nature, mathematical, logical, physical, sensuously pleasing, spiritually valuable, all this must mean for me only something that I have to express in the fashion of ideas. The more I am to know my world, the more of a mind I must have for the purpose. The closer I come to the truth about the things, the more ideas I get. . . . Then reflect. What can, after all, so well agree with an idea as another idea? To what can things that go on in my mind conform unless it be to another mind? If the more my mind grows in mental clearness, the nearer it gets to the nature of reality, then surely the reality that my mind thus resembles must be in itself mental." Royce, *The Spirit of Modern Philosophy* (Boston: Houghton Mifflin Co., 1892), pp. 360–361.
14. Karl Barth, *Dogmatics in Outline*, tr. G. T. Thomson (New York: Philosophical Library, 1949), p. 23.
15. It is only fair to observe that honest thinkers oppose this view of the rationality of the real on the ground that it goes beyond experience; that we have therefore no warrant for such a claim. Such rationality as we find in the world may be the product of our own understanding (Kant), in which case we have no right to dogmatize about the *Ding an sich*. It may be thoroughly alien to our human

ideas. Or we may have derived only such aspects of the real as are commensurate with our mental forms, even as the eye and ear catch only a limited range of colors and pitches. In this case the remainder may be utterly foreign to thought. Or, as F. R. Tennant has shown in his *Philosophical Theology*, Vol. II, chap. 3, the world may be rational in some senses, irrational in others. To all these a common reply can be made. We have here, as Royce observed, one of those perfect dilemmas which delight philosophy. This unintelligible remainder that is now beyond all thought, this *x*, is either accessible to thought, *or* it belongs to that class of things that can only be referred to by such an absurd question as "What is that whole number that is the square root of 65?" Royce, *op. cit.*, pp. 363–368.

16. *Op. cit.*, pp. 305–306.   17. *Op. cit.*, p. 502 (marg. p. 623).
18. *Ibid.*, p. 503 (marg. p. 625).
19. *Ibid.*, p. 505 (marg. p. 627).
20. *Ibid.*, p. 506 (marg. p. 630).
21. *The Fitness of the Environment* (New York: The Macmillan Co., 1913), p. 101.
22. *Ibid.*, p. 272.
23. *Ibid.*, p. 311. The high solubility of water, for example, is now known to be due to the marked electric charges in the corners of the water molecule.
24. In his *Philosophical Theology*, Vol. II (Cambridge: The University Press, 1937).
25. *Ibid.*, p. 82.   26. *Ibid.*, p. 104.
27. *Op. cit.*, p. 663 (marg. p. 826).

CHAPTER 4

1. *The Varieties of Religious Experience* (New York: Longmans, Green & Co., 1902), p. 456.
2. *Ibid.*, p. 456.   3. *Ibid.*, p. 508.
4. *Social Idealism and the Changing Theology* (New York: The Macmillan Co., 1913), p. 239.
5. *Mark* 14:36.
6. *The Essence of Christianity*, tr. Marian Evans (London: John Chapman, 1854), p. 97.
7. *Ibid.*, p. 45.   8. *Ibid.*, p. 122.

9. *Ibid.*, p. 126.   10. *Ibid.*, p. 173.

11. Bennett, *op. cit.*, p. 113.

12. *The Religious Aspect of Philosophy* (Boston: Houghton Mifflin & Co., 1885), p. 12.

13. *A Common Faith* (New Haven: Yale University Press, 1934), p. 51.

14. *Ibid.*, p. 54.   15. *Ibid.*, p. 53.

16. *Ibid.*, p. 51.

17. *The Source of Human Good* (Chicago: The University of Chicago Press, 1946), pp. 264–265.

18. *Ibid.*, p. 265.   19. Dewey, *op. cit.*, p. 31.

20. *The Problem of Religious Knowledge* (New York: Harper & Brothers, 1940), p. 164.

21. *Ibid.*, p. 165.   22. *Ibid.*, p. 170.

23. *Ibid.*, p. 171.   24. *Ibid.*, p. 172.

25. *Ibid.*, p. 173.   26. *Ibid.*, pp. 203–204.

27. *Ibid.*, p. 209.   28. *Ibid.*, p. 209.

29. *Ibid.*, p. 358.   30. *Ibid.*, p. 366.

31. *Ibid.*, p. 367.   32. *Ibid.*, p. 373.

33. *Ibid.*, p. 368.   34. *Ibid.*, p. 381.

35. *Is There a God?* (New York: Harper & Brothers), p. 292.

36. In *The Nature of Religious Experience*, ed. J. S. Bixler (New York: Harper & Brothers, 1937), chapter 3.

37. Few empiricists would admit such a limitation. They profess to seek only what can be verified in experience, with scientific experience being given priority. But their postulates are not subject to this kind of verification. Indeed, the "pretense" of empiricism is always to be found in the unanalyzed presuppositions on which they build their argument. The attempt of some empiricists to define meaning as the logical relation of sentences, without any reference to internal meaning, simply breaks down. Cf. esp. William Henry Werkmeister, *The Basis and Structure of Knowledge* (New York: Harper & Brothers, 1948), pp. 29–30, 40–44.

38. Richard Niebuhr in *The Nature of Religious Experience*, p. 101.

39. *Theology as an Empirical Science* (New York: The Macmillan Co., 1919), p. 120.

40. *Ibid.*, p. 168.

41. *Ibid.*, p. 169. This is the Kantian (moral) statement of forgiveness. It reappears often since Kant's day, as for example in Henry Nelson Wieman, *Religious Experience and Scientific Method* (New York: The Macmillan Co., 1926), pp. 102–104.

42. Royce, *The Problem of Christianity* (New York: The Macmillan Co., 1916), Vol. II, pp. 260–261.

43. *Romans* 5:10.   44. *Romans* 3:26.

45. *John* 9:25.   46. *Psalm* 34:8.

47. *Malachi* 3:10.   48. *Psalm* 103:2–5.

49. *Luke* 7:22.

CHAPTER 5

1. *Nein!* (Munich: Chr. Kaiser, 1934), pp. 12–13. This pamphlet and Brunner's *Natur und Gnade* have been translated into English by Peter Fraenkel and are available in a small volume entitled *Natural Theology* (London: Geoffrey Bles, The Centenary Press, 1946). The translations from these two pamphlets contained in this chapter are my own.

2. *Natur und Gnade* (Tuebingen: B. Mohr [Paul Siebeck] 1935), p. 18.

3. *Ibid.*, p. 20.   4. *Nein!*, pp. 16–17.

5. *Dogmatics in Outline*, p. 16.   6. *Romans* 1:19–20.

7. *Commentary on Romans*, tr. from 6th edition by Edwyn C. Hoskins (New York: Oxford University Press, 1933), pp. 45–46.

8. *Dogmatics in Outline*, p. 22.   9. *Ibid.*, p. 11.

10. *Natur und Gnade*, p. 43.   11. *Nein!* p. 62.

12. *Dogmatics in Outline*, p. 31.   13. *Ibid.*, p. 32.

14. *Ibid.*, p. 33.   15. *Nein!* p. 62.

16. *Christianity and Philosophy*, tr. Ralph Macdonald (New York: Sheed and Ward, 1939), p. 80.

17. *Institutes*, tr. John Allen (Philadelphia: The Westminster Press, 1936), Vol. I, pp. 77–78.

18. *Op. cit.*, p. 35.

19. Walter Farrell, *A Companion to the Summa*, Vol. I (New York: Sheed and Ward, 1941), p. 29.

20. St. Augustine, *On the Freedom of the Will*, tr. Francis E. Tourscher (Philadelphia: Peter Reilly Company, 1937), Book II, chap. 2.

21. Gilson, *op. cit.*, p. 66.

22. R. P. Phillips, *Modern Thomistic Philosophy* (London: Burns, Oates and Washbourne, Ltd., 1935; American Edition, 1946, by the Newman Press, Westminster, Maryland), Vol. II, p. 280.

23. *Summa Theologica*, translated by Dominican Fathers, 3rd edition

(London: Burns, Oates and Washbourne, Ltd., 1911; New York: Benziger Brothers, Inc.), Vol. I, p. 25.

24. Brother Benignus (Gerrity), *Nature, Knowledge and God* (Milwaukee: The Bruce Publishing Company, 1947), chap. 21.

25. Farrell, *op. cit.*, p. 36. 26. *Summa Theologica*, Vol. I, p. 26.

27. Brother Benignus, *op. cit.*, chap. 21.

28. Phillips, *op. cit.*, Vol. II, p. 289.

CHAPTER 6

1. William James saw this clearly. "So long as we deal with the cosmic and the general, we deal only with the symbols of reality, but *as soon as we deal with private and personal phenomena as such, we deal with realities in the completest sense of the term.* . . . The individual's religion may be egoistic, and those private realities which it keeps in touch with may be narrow enough; but at any rate it always remains infinitely less hollow and abstract, as far as it goes, than a science which prides itself on taking no account of anything private at all." *The Varieties of Religious Experience*, pp. 498, 500.

2. For the concept of probability see any good recent textbook in Logic or Introduction to Philosophy. While science now recognizes that many of its findings are in terms of probability rather than exactness, the degrees of probability are stated in fractions. A probability of $8/10$ is preferable to one of $7/10$. The purpose is to raise the fraction of probability toward the number 1 as a limit. The mathematical ideal persists.

3. *The Nicomachaean Ethics*, Book I, sec. 3.

4. Royce, *The Conception of God*, p. 33.

5. *The World and the Individual*, Vol. II, p. 172.

6. Thus Hocking: "The hermit, the lonely sheep-driver, is likely to succumb to his illusions, living with them in preference to the world which we of the majority call real. . . . The 'established character' of Nature is sharpest where men are thickest, is clearly some function of the volume of our empirical conversation: it gives the impression of being a consensus effect." *The Meaning of God in Human Experience*, p. 293.

7. *Studies of Good and Evil* (New York: D. Appleton & Co., 1898), p. 208.

8. *I Corinthians* 2:11.   9. *The Primacy of Faith*, p. 159.

10. *Job* 38:4.   11. *Ephesians* 4:18.

12. *I Corinthians* 2:14.   13. *John* 13:34.

14. *I Corinthians* 13:6, 7 (New York: Harper & Brothers, 1922).

15. An illuminating example is found in the American government's release of stories of enemy atrocities just before each of the war bond drives in the last war. Here resentment against the enemy was deliberately fostered, as well as reassurance about the rightness of our own cause.

16. *Micah* 4:3.

17. For an excellent treatment of the fanatical pretensions of both Roman and Protestant churches, cf. Reinhold Niebuhr, *The Nature and Destiny of Man*, Vol. II, pp. 220–231.

18. *Ends and Means* (New York: Harper & Brothers, 1937), p. 312.

CHAPTER 7

1. *Psalm* 139:16.   2. *I Corinthians* 2:11.

3. Cf. Whitehead's distinction between the "primordial" and the "consequent nature of God" in *Process and Reality* (New York: The Macmillan Co., 1929), pp. 521–533.

4. In the *Phaedo*.

5. Act III (New York: Coward-McCann, Inc., 1938), p. 83.

6. *Genesis* 3:4, marginal translation.

7. *Romans* 3:26, American Standard Version, italics mine.

8. *Isaiah* 1:2.

9. Emil Brunner, *Revelation and Reason*, tr. Olive Wyon (Philadelphia: The Westminster Press, 1946), p. 105.

10. *Matthew* 11:28.

11. *The Meaning of God in Human Experience*, p. 229.

12. *Galatians* 2:20.   13. *John* 7:17.

14. *Matthew* 11:25.   15. *I Corinthians* 1:17.

16. *I Corinthians* 1:21.   17. *I Corinthians* 3:19.

18. *The Critique of Pure Reason*, p. 665 (marg. p. 829).

19. Wieman, H. N. and Meland, B. E., *American Philosophies of Religion* (New York: Harper & Brothers, 1936), p. 87.

20. L. P. Jacks, *Religious Perplexities* (New York: Harper & Brothers, 1923), pp. 32–33.

21. Karl Barth, *Dogmatics in Outline*, p. 20.
22. Reinhold Niebuhr, *The Nature and Destiny of Man*, Vol. II, p. 243.

CHAPTER 8

1. *Deuteronomy* 5:6.   2. *Isaiah* 1:5–7.
3. Chapter 5.   4. *Hosea* 2:14.
5. Paul Tillich, "What is Wrong with 'Dialectic' Theology," *Journal of Religion*, Vol. XV, p. 140.
6. *The Varieties of Religious Experience*, p. 519.

CHAPTER 9

1. *James* 2:19.
2. Cf. Charles T. Seltman, *Attic Vase-Painting* (Cambridge: Harvard University Press, 1933), pp. 74–75. The thesis is offered that the year 454 B.C., when the Treasury of the Delian Confederacy was transferred to Athens, also marks the beginning of decline in Greek art. "Athens made the great betrayal, and so her art first slowly changed to artificiality, and then drooped to degeneration." P. 75.
3. Reinhold Niebuhr, *The Nature and Destiny of Man*, Vol. II, p. 223.
4. Alfred North Whitehead, *Religion in the Making* (New York: The Macmillan Co., 1926), p. 88.
5. Unpublished papers.
6. Robert Browning, "Rabbi ben Ezra."
7. Reprinted from *I Believe*, edited by Clifton Fadiman. (New York: Simon and Schuster, Inc., 1939), pp. 347–348.
8. *Jeremiah* 2:13.   9. *Luke* 15:17.
10. C. G. Jung, *Modern Man in Search of a Soul*, tr. W. S. Dell and Cary F. Baynes (New York: Harcourt, Brace and Co., 1933), pp. 39–40.
11. *Institutes*, Vol. I, p. 47.

Index of Subjects

Anxiety, 13, 76, 116-117, 142
Apologetics, defects of, 5-6, 148
Atonement, 71-73, 85, 117-118, 123

Bible, inspiration of, 123-129, 141-143
Biblical research, 125-126, 141-143

Collectivism, 153, 154-160
Communication, 1-2, 4, 80-83, 98-99, 131, 133-134, 138
Communism, 150
Cosmological argument, 6, 44-45, 86-89
Creation, 113-114, 116

Death, 13, 14, 114-116, 132, 143
Dialectical theology, 43, 134
Doubt, implying truth, 12-13

Economics, 17, 27, 43, 95, 141, 145, 153, 154, 159, 160
Empirical theology, 60-62, 64-74
Empiricism, 16-17, 20-21, 53-54, 58-60, 68, 70, 73-74, 86, 94
Encounter, personal, 90, 96-103, 112-113, 120-122, 123, 129, 130, 134, 135, 140, 141, 143, 148, 152, 153, 161-162
Ethics, 26, 28, 31, 50-51, 66-67, 107, 143-146, 156-157
Evolution, 45-47
Existential knowledge, 31, 98-103, 120, 121, 128, 147, 162
Existentialism, 149

Faith, as belief, 67, 89-90, 121-122, 124, 127; as gift of Holy Spirit, 77, 78, 120-121, 129, 134-135, 142; as hypothesis, 67-68; as irrational, 6, 9; as knowledge, 100-101, 120-122; as valor, 122-123; inseparable from

reason, 32, 83, 103-104, 131, 148; objective intent of, 3-4, 9, 57, 68, 78-79, 83, 102-104, 131; saving, 78, 118, 120, 122, 125, 126, 131, 145, 146; suspicious of reason, 5-8
Fear, 13, 74, 110, 117, 132, 136, 161
Freedom, political, 155-160
Forgiveness, 51, 59, 70-73, 74, 108, 112, 116, 117-118, 121, 128, 161

God, as Creator, 49, 109, 113-114; as private symbol, 3-4; as unknown, 1, 29, 79, 92, 123; attributes of, 55-56, 63, 85, 88-89, 104, 123; "proofs" of existence, 5-6, 36-52, 76, 84-89, 112, 131, 147
Grace, 51, 71, 72-73, 76, 78, 83, 105, 117-118, 119, 122, 123, 125, 129, 131, 133, 143, 145, 146, 150, 161-162

Humanism, 55-56, 58, 155-157

Idealism, 40, 42, 109, 110
Idolatry, 8, 17, 75, 76, 77, 116, 124, 126-127, 131, 159
Immortality, 50, 56, 63, 114-116, 132
Incarnation, 85, 133-134
Individualism, 23-24, 152-155, 159
Individuation, principle of, 28-31
Injustice, 117, 142, 144, 145, 146, 149
Instrumentalism, 18-19
Internal meaning, 19-33, 34, 50-51, 54, 83, 90, 95, 101-102, 115, 120, 131, 148, 152

Jesus, as example, 63, 70, 71, 78; as Son of God, 63, 118; as teacher, 133; the historical, 63; uniqueness of, 63, 70-71

Index of Names

Sperto

Colony